D1174179

Tending the Garden State

Tending the Garden State

Preserving New Jersey's Farming Legacy

CHARLES H. HARRISON

Rivergate Books
an imprint of Rutgers University Press
New Brunswick, New Jersey, and London

Library of Congress Cataloging-in-Publication Data

Harrison, Charles Hampton, 1932–
    Tending the garden state : preserving New Jersey's farming legacy /
Charles H. Harrison.
        p. cm.
    Includes bibliographical references and index.
    ISBN-13: 978–0–8135–3906–5 (hardcover : alk. paper)
    1. Agriculture—New Jersey—History. I. Title.
    S451.N55.H37   2006
    630.9749—dc22

                                                    2006007085

A British Cataloging-in-Publication record for this book is available from the
British Library.

The publication of this volume has been made possible, in part, by a
gift from Nicholas G. Rutgers IV and Nancy Hall Rutgers to support
books about New Jersey.

CONTENTS 🌿

PROLOGUE 🌺

In 1684, a publicist, presumably acting on behalf of landowners in the twenty-year-old British colony across the sea, papered Scotland with posters urging restless Scots to leave their lowlands and highlands and embark for the "Province of New East Jersey, a pleasant and profitable country," which, he boasted, "belongs to Scotsmen."

As any good PR consultant or ad agent knows, it doesn't hurt to get an endorsement from some well-known person. One such celebrity in late seventeenth century England was the London mapmaker John Ogilby, who, in his world atlas, had referred to the colony as a place "where the land floweth with milk and honey." Not content with Ogilby's paraphrase of Exodus 3:8, the publicist also quoted the noted mapmaker as referring to New East Jersey as the "Garden of the World." So far as historians know, Ogilby never coined that tagline, but today, more than three centuries later, New Jersey, the nation's most urban state, still calls itself a garden. It says so on millions of license plates.

New Jersey officially became the Garden State in December 1954 when the state legislature approved a bill requiring the Division of Motor Vehicles to commence imprinting those words on every license plate beginning with the next issue, scheduled for 1956. It almost didn't happen. A similar bill had been vetoed in 1953 by Republican governor Alfred E. Driscoll, who thought the license plate, being "an important legal device" (representing the automobile's registration), would be compromised by including the motto. A second attempt was vetoed in 1954 by Democratic governor Robert B. Meyner, who stated pointedly, "I do not believe that the average citizen of New Jersey regards his state as more peculiarly identifiable with gardening or farming than any of its other industries or occupations."

Neither Driscoll nor Meyner counted on the persistence of fifty-three-year-old assemblyman C. William Haines, a fruit grower from Burlington County, who was the chief sponsor of both bills. Meyner, in his veto message, also had pointed out that the then current license plate was too small even to accommodate the motto. Haines addressed that complaint when the bill was introduced and passed over Meyner's veto. In a statement to legislators, Haines said the Division of Motor Vehicles would be instructed to increase the size of the license plate "in conformity with recommendations of the Interstate Traffic Code." And so it was done.

Apparently, Meyner also misjudged the "average citizen of New Jersey," because in a November 2004 poll of 906 residents, 85 percent of respondents said farming should play a valuable role in the future of New Jersey. As one reporter observed at the time, New Jersey residents still "have a Garden State of mind," and the headline on his story blared "A populist cry to keep 'Garden' in Garden State." John W. Schiemann, director of research for Public Mind, which conducted the poll, said at the time that he considered it remarkable that 57 percent of respondents connected the slogan Garden State to farming. "For one of the most densely populated states in the union, with its share of urban areas, that's a strikingly high number," he said.

However, 43 percent of the poll's respondents thought the slogan referred to their backyard gardens or window flower boxes, and, alas, it is not uncommon in 2006 for grown-up shoppers to push their supermarket carts past peppers, peaches, and produce of every kind and give not the slightest thought to where those vegetables and fruits came from. Danny Heitman, in a column written for *Smithsonian* magazine, recounted the time he was standing in line at the store when a cashier held up a melon and admitted, "I don't know what to charge you, because I don't know what to call this." Trying to hide his surprise, Heitman responded, "It's called a cantaloupe."

Because of those 426 New Jerseyans who didn't know that the garden in Garden State refers to the farm in the next county over or somewhere downstate, because of cashiers and shoppers who may not know a blueberry from a blackberry, and because out-of-state friends simply refuse to believe my native state is not completely built over and built out, I decided to go in search of the Garden State. I sought to discover what, in fact, remained of the farmland—the agriculture that Assemblyman Haines and his colleagues wanted to call attention to fifty years ago, and what, if anything, was being done to preserve it.

What I learned was occasionally unsettling, often eye-popping, and almost always reassuring that the state of the Garden State is good. Unfortunately, some rich and productive New Jersey farms continue to disappear under cement blocks and macadam, but an increasing number of them have been preserved for all time, and the farmers who own that land are finding new ways to market their products. For example, I tasted peach cider for the first time and walked down rows of mint grown almost exclusively to adorn and embellish exotic rum drinks. Particularly enlightening and encouraging was talking with professional planners, designers, and architects who might otherwise be engaged in concocting great globs of mansions in field, forest, and pasture but are instead creating town centers that provide housing for families who need it while at the same time keep developments from swallowing up farmland.

The February 2005 issue of *Gardener News* intrigued readers with a big, bold headline that read "New Jersey's Best Kept Secret." The secret turned out to be Rutgers University's Agricultural Experiment Station (AES). I have to admit that I was one of countless New Jerseyans for whom AES was a secret, not because the station purposely hid from the public its extraordinary and most beneficial work, but because we weren't paying careful attention. Now, in my search of the Garden State, I paid attention. Finally, behaving like the journalist I have prided myself on being my entire adult, working life, I asked the right questions of the right people, observed and noted all that they had to show me, and came away determined to reveal those wonderful examples of agricultural research and application that often have gone unnoticed and unappreciated through the years.

Above all, perhaps, in my search I encountered many more individuals than I might have expected who not only care very deeply about the Garden State and preserving New Jersey's farming legacy but who are every day making it possible for that legacy not only to be passed on to future generations, but for the legacy to be enhanced and enlarged by them. People like David Duffield and his sons, daughter, and daughters-in-law in Washington Township, Gloucester County. They not only have preserved and prospered one of the only remaining farms in that Philadelphia suburb, but they teach hundreds of schoolchildren each year how to plant seeds, grow and harvest vegetables from those seeds, and, most of all, how to appreciate the rich earth and what comes from it. People like the Sussex County dairymen who pretty much ignored all the signs that the dairy business in New Jersey was all but kaput and joined together to produce and market a higher grade of milk than is now available in most stores in most states. People like the elderly but spry Minnie Ware of Salem County, who lives in a house that's almost three hundred years old and continues to manage a farm that has been productive even longer.

After three years of reading, listening, and looking, I have come away from the search convinced that so long as enough men and women love the land enough to defend and work it, New Jersey will remain true to its decades-old motto born of a centuries-old quotation. The Garden State is alive and lively and looking to the future with well-founded hope and, even better, a resolute commitment to the legacy.

Tending the Garden State

"A Pleasant and Profitable Country"

CHAPTER 1

W hen the Dutch crossed the Hudson River from Manhattan in the early decades of the seventeenth century to settle what is now Bergen County, they discovered hills of corn and beans planted by Minsi natives of the Leni-Lenape tribe. And when the Quaker land speculator John Fenwick walked down the gangplank from the English ship *Griffin* in 1675 and set foot in what is today Salem County, he found Unalachtigo natives of the same tribe gathering wild cranberries and feasting on oysters and clams they had brought back with them after spending the summer at the shore.

The gardens of the Garden State go back that far—and perhaps a lot farther, to whatever time the Leni-Lenape (meaning the Original People) drifted east past the Appalachian bumps along the upper Delaware River and spread south into the flatlands that end where the same river joins the sea. The search—the farming legacy—begins, then, with the Leni-Lenape tribe, a branch of the Algonquian nation, a generally peaceful people whom the more contentious Iroquois derided as "old women."

It was the Leni-Lenape women, old and young, who tended the gardens. They were not gardens the newcomers from Europe would ordinarily recognize, because the women cared little about neat

1

rows and symmetry. This early farming typically began in a clearing outside the village that had been created when a stand of trees earlier girdled by men had died and been brought down and burned.

The women scratched the earth with a crooked stick, crudely honed stone hoe, or perhaps the shoulder blade of a deer tied to a tree branch. Corn and beans were planted in the same hills because, to the women, it was a no-brainer that the beans would be easier to pick if their vines clung to the corn stalks. The women also planted pumpkins or squash and strong, not very good tobacco. The Original People had no book knowledge about fertilization and crop rotation; however, they knew that fish heads worked into the soil helped grow taller corn, and they sensed that when the garden began yielding inferior crops, it was time to start another garden.

Women not only worked the gardens, they also gathered wild persimmons, grapes, huckleberries, blackberries, beach plums, varieties of herbs and nuts, and strawberries. The men, for their part, were responsible for hunting and fishing. This division of labor was understood by a Leni-Lenape couple from the start. The bridegroom presented his new wife with a bone from an animal he had brought down with bow and arrow, and the bride gave as her gift to him an ear of corn she had picked from the garden she tended.[1]

For a great many years before the arrival of the Europeans, the Original People and the land they lived on coexisted harmoniously. The natives planted their crops in the spring, enjoyed the fruits of the ocean in summer, harvested crops in the fall, and hunted animals for their meat in the winter. The early Dutch and English settlers—and all the generations of farmers since—learned valuable lessons from the Leni-Lenape. It has been estimated that one-third of modern American agricultural products and practices may be of Native American origin.[2]

The Dutch Farm Their Bouweries

In the year 1629, the Dutch West India Company encouraged emigration from Holland and settlement in the province of New Netherland, which included a wide swath of fertile ground across the Hudson River from New Amsterdam and spreading west from the imposing Palisades. The Dutch called this stretch of New Netherland "Bergen." The objective of the Dutch West India Company was to develop agricultural communities. The company stated that it appreciated the Indians' claim to the soil, but its primary aim was to encourage white, immigrant farmers to settle the land. Furthermore, the company promised to protect those farmers in the event the Original People might want to exercise their claim and take back a piece of the land they didn't realize they had given away in the first place.[3]

The Dutch who settled Bergen and elsewhere called their farms, or plantations, "bouweries." On these farms they grew, of course, the beans, corn, and pumpkins to which the native women had introduced them. They added familiar crops imported from the Netherlands: cabbages, parsnips, carrots, beets, spinach, onions, leeks, artichokes, and asparagus.[4] A Dutch writer by the name of VanderDonck, after touring some of the bouweries, noted that his countrymen were growing "every kind of garden vegetable, which thrive and yield well."[5]

However, farmers newly arrived from Holland had to adjust and improvise. Canals and ditches back home that kept livestock corralled did not exist in Bergen, and wandering horses and cows tended to antagonize the natives and also lead to indiscriminate and untimely breeding, so the farmers had to build fences. They also had to choose which Leni-Lenape agricultural practices they would adopt and which ones they would reject. For example, the Dutch did not care much for the native practice of girdling trees to clear land for planting; the newcomers preferred to chop down trees and all other growth as quickly as possible. They did latch on to the native women's scheme whereby bean vines curled up corn stalks, but instead of planting the seeds together on one hill, as the native women did, they first planted corn in precise rows six inches apart, European style; then, when the stalks were roughly six inches high, they plunked down pole beans close to the hills of corn. The new farmers did continue for some time the Indians' practice of burning off the forests.[6]

✽ New Netherland Becomes New Jersey

As New Netherland welcomed the sixth decade of the seventeenth century, the production from the Bergen farms of Albert Van Voorhys, Volckert Van Noorstrant, Cornelius Vanderwerf, and other

Dutch settlers was bountiful indeed. Then, one harvest day in the autumn of 1664, they awoke at the squawk of the rooster to discover that New Netherland had become New Jersey. What had happened, in fairly quick succession for those times, was that Charles II of England decided to take New Netherland away from the Dutch and give it to his brother, the Duke of York. The Duke set sail almost immediately with a fleet boasting enough armament to blast away Dutch forts at the tip of Manhattan Island and on either shore of the Delaware Bay, if such bombardment became necessary (it didn't). While still aboard ship in the middle of the Atlantic, the duke, in a moment of extreme generosity, gave away New Jersey to his buddies, Sir John Berkeley and Sir George Carteret. It was because of Carteret's defense of the Isle of Jersey against the forces of Oliver Cromwell that all the land between the rivers Hudson and Delaware was named New Jersey. However, there was an embarrassing moment when Colonel Richard Nicolls, who headed the duke's expedition and later became governor of New York and New Jersey, became confused and called New Jersey "Albania" (the duke was of York and Albany), but that's another story.[7]

Ten years after the English displaced the Dutch, Lord Berkeley lost interest in governing his piece of New Jersey, which included most of the land that later became West Jersey, and he agreed to sell his share to a Quaker named John Fenwick. The asking price was one thousand pounds sterling. In the end, Fenwick could only afford to buy a portion of the land offered by Lord Berkeley, with most of the purchase price consisting of down payments from fifty or so wealthy men who, together, bought 140,000 acres in what was to become Salem and Cumberland Counties.[8]

When a tentative date to set sail for America was fixed, Fenwick went all over London buying supplies for the voyage and to sustain his party of settlers until they could subsist on their own. Unfortunately, he charged most of his purchases. When his creditors got wind of what he was doing, they demanded payment, which, of course, he didn't have. In desperation, Fenwick turned to John Eldridge and Edmund Warner, also Quakers, who said they would pay off his debts in return for mortgages on some of the land already purchased. Fenwick had no choice but to go along.[9]

The Friends, Eldridge and Warner, turned out to be not such good friends. After Fenwick's arrival in New Salem, he learned that

Eldridge and Warner did not, after all, pay off his debts, but instead circulated the story in London that Fenwick really didn't own any land in America because they held the mortgages.[10] Whereas most of the later land grants in West Jersey were between two hundred and five hundred acres and, in East Jersey, slightly less than that, some of the individual land acquisitions in Fenwick's colony numbered in the thousands of acres. For example, John Addams and Samuel Hedge each farmed two thousand acres, and Fenwick reserved six thousand acres for himself.

The farmland in Elsinboro west of Salem City and east of the Delaware River, which today is planted mostly in soybeans, has brought forth a grain or vegetable crop every season since the Leni-Lenape native women tended their corn, beans, and tobacco. Once included in Fenwick's colony, for a few years beginning in 1641 the land was home to a small band of New England Puritans who staked a claim as the New Haven Colony. Alas, most of the Puritans were driven out in 1644 by a deadly combination of Johan Printz, who for a time governed a settlement of Swedes along the river, rampant viral infections, and voracious mosquitoes.

For the last 285 years, crops have been harvested and history witnessed by residents of the patterned brick house that is set back nearly a tenth of a mile from Amwellbury Road in Elsinboro. The side of the two-story house that faces the road displays what historians have called the finest example of diaper (diamond) design of any patterned brick house in Salem County. At the top of that wall, spelled out in brick headers (ends) glazed white, is the date when Joseph Darkin built the house—1720.

The current owner of the house is Minnie Willis Ware, a diminutive woman of advanced years who wouldn't surprise anyone if she rolled up her sleeves and worked side by side with the men planting seed in the spring. Her husband, Preston, who died in 1999, was descended from early settlers (an ancestor was aboard the *Griffin* with Fenwick), and at one time he was president of the New Jersey State Board of Agriculture and a member of the board of the American Soybean Association. On a dining room wall in the house is a plaque that announces Preston as the 1972 winner of the annual Rutgers Soils and Crops Department award for highest soybean yield: 60.8 bushels per acre.

The Ware family, which includes Minnie, son Lee, and the widow of son Clinton, together now farms 160 acres. While the current cash crop is soybeans, the Wares over the years have planted okra, asparagus, tomatoes, and bell peppers. One bright summer day a while back, Minnie Ware stood under a giant sycamore planted by her husband and looked over the fields that have been tilled so long by so many. "I remember taking truckloads of tomatoes to the processing plants (principally Heinz and Ritter). What a shame, all those plants are now gone."

But not the land. Never the land.

✻ When North and South Were East and West

Today, New Jerseyans separate themselves into North Jersey and South Jersey, with the unofficial divider understood to be Interstate 195, which runs from Trenton in the west to Belmar in the east. The year after Fenwick and his settlers arrived, New Jersey was separated by royal decree into East Jersey and West Jersey. The two provinces were divided by a line extending from the Delaware Water Gap in the northwest to Little Egg Harbor in the southeast. The capital of East Jersey was at Perth Amboy, and the province included the better part of what had been New Netherland. Burlington became the capital of West Jersey, which included the biggest bulge in the kidney-shaped state; for example, the distance across the state from Salem to Little Egg Harbor, the ending point for the east/west demarcation line, is about seventy miles as the crow or seagull flies.

As more and more families—primarily English, Scottish, Irish, and a smattering of German—immigrated to the two provinces, they slowly filled in the land and made it their own. The earliest settlers planted a variety of crops in an effort to determine which of them grew best in the soil they were not accustomed to. The farmers eliminated strains that did not do well and saved seed from those that did best. For example, they alternately planted corn, wheat, rye, oats, barley, and peas. Some vegetables and fruits that European settlers brought with them from the old country fared rather well in American soil. Cabbage was one of those imports that liked New Jersey soil from the beginning, and it could be found in nearly every settler's garden. Most new farmers also planted an apple orchard.[11]

A letter written at Burlington in 1680 by Mahlon Stacy, who was visiting his brother Robert, provides an eyewitness account of farming in West Jersey in the late seventeenth century:

> I have seen orchards laden with fruit to admiration, their very limbs torn to pieces with the weight, and most delicious to the taste, and lovely to behold. . . . I have seen and known this summer, forty bushels of bold wheat of one bushel sown. . . . We have from the time called May until Michaelmas [a feast held in late September to honor the archangel Michael] great store of very good wild fruits, as strawberries, cranberries, and hurtleberries [probably huckleberries], which are like our bilberries in England but far sweeter; they are very wholesome fruits. It is my judgment by what I have observed that fruit trees in this country destroy themselves by the very weight of their fruit.[12]

Across the colony, and closer to the Atlantic coast, the proprietors of East Jersey, hoping to promote emigration to their province, published their list of top fifteen reasons why a European family should give up whatever life it had grown accustomed to at home and embark on the long and often treacherous voyage to a new and distant land still populated by bronze-colored men and women whose dress, language, and customs could not be more foreign.

The first four reasons boasted of a good climate, safe harbors, and great fishing. Five and six told of "lovely springs, rivulets, inland rivers and creeks" and a great variety of trees. Number seven advertised land "varied in goodness and richness, but generally fertile . . . it produceth plentiful crops of all sorts." Reasons eight and nine were devoted to listing all the animals that could either be hunted or herded and the great number of delicious fruits that the immigrant family would discover growing wild on bushes and trees. Most of the remaining reasons tended to repeat and add PR luster to previous claims. However, number twelve described the kinds of people and skills that would most likely succeed and be most welcome in America. For example: "industrious husbandmen" who didn't mind "hard labor," and all manner of craftsmen.[13]

As New Jersey came into the eighteenth century, the majority of its residents were farmers living in tiny farming communities. In place of the hunter-gatherer relationship that had served the Leni-Lenape for centuries, the recent immigrants transplanted from Europe were organized as farming families; the man of the Dutch *haus* could be found more often in the garden with a hoe in his hand than in the woods with a rifle over his shoulder. Also, the farming families of the new century were no longer content, as the Native Americans and even their forebears had been, to raise crops almost exclusively for their own use. While New Jersey farms had produced vegetables since the Dutch introduced cabbage into their gardens in the middle of the seventeenth century, in the decades before the American Revolution vegetables were grown in limited quantities for market. This was the small beginning that eventually led to New Jersey's becoming the great garden serving New York and Philadelphia and all the towns in between—and not a few villages beyond those cities. At this early stage, cabbage was still the vegetable of greatest commercial importance; it was used primarily to make sauerkraut. In the middle of the century, large quantities of cabbage were grown in South Jersey as well as in Bergen and Hudson Counties, and by 1770, it was reported that cabbages were cultivated by almost every farming family in the colony. Whole fields were common. Watermelons and turnips were also grown for market.[14]

New Jersey became the most prolific provider of any colony or province in North America, supplying vast quantities of flour, beef, pork, horses, and vegetables to its neighbors and beyond. Farmers in the northwestern part of the colony floated grain down the Delaware River on flatboats destined for Philadelphia docks. Exports from Perth Amboy recorded at the time included "8,906 bushels of Indian corn . . . 350 bushels of bran, 50 bushels of potatoes . . . 25 bushels of turnips, 1000 ropes of onions . . . and 55 barrels of apples."[15]

❧ Breadbasket of the American Revolution

In the eighteenth century, New Jersey was known as the corridor between Philadelphia and New York (and a connection between colonies/states in New England and the South). Of course, it still is, and the turnpike laid down in the twentieth century simply allows many more horses to travel the same distance in a fraction of the time required in the 1700s. Because of its nearness to these primary centers of political and economic power in eighteenth-century America, New Jersey also became the most embattled colony during the American Revolution, and, most crucial to our present consideration, its rich farms became the breadbasket for the contending armies and their supporting units of Whigs (patriots) and Tories (loyalists).

In prewar Bergen County, the primarily Dutch farmers were in a quandary. Their hearts, or at least some of them, might have been sympathetic to the views of those radicals who advocated breaking all ties with Great Britain, but their heads reminded them that the local agricultural economy was largely dependent on commerce with British-controlled New York City. Therefore, the blockade of Boston Harbor by the British in June 1774 sent an unwelcome message to these farmers and posed a troubling question: suppose the British government decided to make New York City off limits to Bergen farmers marketing their produce, beef, and grain.

It was not surprising, therefore, that most of Bergen County's farmers supported a peaceful solution to the dispute between the colonies and Great Britain. At a meeting of more than three hundred residents of Bergen County, held in Hackensack in 1774, a resolution was passed that affirmed residents' loyalty to the king, but also called for the election of delegates to a colonial congress that would petition Parliament to end its "ruinous administration of the colonial economy."[16]

Two years later, of course, a peaceful resolution between the colonies and Great Britain was no longer possible. On June 29, 1776, nearly on the eve of the Continental Congress's declaring independence, and with the flowers of prosperous Dutch farms in full bloom, David Baulding, a Bergen blacksmith, stopped off for a toddy at the Three Pidgeons Tavern on his way into the city. Another patron, anxious to be the bearer of big tidings, told Baulding that he "had it on good authority" that as many as one hundred British ships were off Sandy Hook and on their way into New York Harbor. For once, barroom gossip turned out to be reliable intelligence. Those ships did sail into the harbor, and most of them were transports, their decks colored crimson with thousands of redcoats.[17]

For the duration of the war, Bergen County continued to trade with British authorities in New York. Not only were the occupational army and the loyalists they protected a prime market, but they also paid in gold. However, patriot militia often interfered with that trade, and when that happened, the British ferried troops across the Hudson with a dual purpose: to attack and destroy the patriot militia and to forage for whatever the king's army needed in the way of food and anything else it wanted.[18]

Sir Henry Clinton launched just such a major foraging expedition out of New York in September 1777. American general Alexander McDougall, with a small number of soldiers under his command, could do little more than watch the redcoats and Hessians strip Bergen farms and farmhouses. According to McDougall's report, the raiding party carted off two hundred cattle, an equal number of sheep (presumably for the mutton), a vast amount of produce, and as many useful items from people's homes as they could carry. Dutch farmers who remained loyal to the Crown lost as much as those who sided with the American cause. Clinton later boasted that his soldiers took whatever "afforded a seasonable refreshment [and] without costing either them [the army] or the government a shilling."[19]

The British were aided by loyalist companies that conducted foraging raids out of fortifications, or blockhouses, along the Palisades. Over a period of months, one such company wandered the countryside, taking from farmer families whatever they wanted; if these plunderers suspected a farming family was sympathetic to the patriot cause, they would most likely burn the family's homestead as well.[20]

Unfortunately for the farmers, they did not fare much better at the hands of the Continental Army and its patriot militias. In the fall of 1779, American general Anthony Wayne, whose troops had just conducted a successful attack on British troops at Stony Point, New York, moved into Paramus, Bergen County, and filled sixty to one hundred wagons with farm produce. The army then moved south in Bergen County, where it gathered one hundred cattle and a considerable amount of grain. One of Wayne's staff officers wrote of the American soldiers: "They have indiscriminately stripped the neighbors of their corn, milk, ducks, fowls, etc." After Wayne's men departed the area, even farmers who sympathized with the patriots must have wondered whether they were any better off with the Continental Army than they were with the redcoats.[21]

A year earlier, Wayne had led a foraging party into Salem County that, by some accounts, helped save the Continental Army then encamped and starving at Valley Forge. In February 1778, Wayne's force crossed the frozen Delaware River just below Wilmington, Delaware. They rounded up 150 cattle from the Quaker farmers in Salem County and embarked on a cattle drive north through Gloucester County into Burlington County, where they halted in the vicinity of Mount Holly. They crossed back over the Delaware and arrived at Valley Forge in time to prevent widespread starvation among the troops. Without the Salem County cattle, it is doubtful whether Washington and the Continental Army could have remained at Valley Forge.[22]

The Quakers of West Jersey were almost unanimously antiwar but not necessarily anti-American. Like the Dutch farmers of East Jersey who continued to trade with the British in New York, many Quaker farmers sold the bounty from their farms to the British while they occupied Philadelphia from the fall of 1777 to late spring of 1778. Again, as was true up north, when the British were not satisfied with what they could purchase from farmers, they sent out troops in force to secure whatever else they desired. Foraging expeditions also were designed to confront and destroy patriot militia wherever they were found and to punish farmers and others whom the British suspected of aiding the militia.

The King's Highway, built in the late seventeenth century, was the main road uniting the communities of West Jersey. It ran from Burlington, the capital of West Jersey and a port on the upper Delaware, southwest to the port of Salem, which is situated just before the river begins a wide turn south to become Delaware Bay. Margaret and Clement Hall owned a farm along the King's Highway near Salem; unfortunately for them, their neighbor was Colonel Benjamin Holme, one of the commanders of the patriot militia that patrolled Salem and Cumberland counties. The Holme farmstead was a frequent target of British and Tory raids; on one occasion, British troops under the command of Colonel Charles Mawhood set a fire in the Holme house that nearly gutted it.

Margaret Hall kept a record of everything the British and Tories (also called refugees) stole from her and her husband. Here are examples of her entries:

Taken . . . when the British Fleet came up the River, ye 7th month 1777, by sailors from on board the fleet: 42 geese. ducks and fowls; 1 shoat, about 50 pounds; 4 bags almost new; a cheese about 14 wt. and cheese fast and several cheese cloths; a brass kettle, held about 4 gallons; a new frying pan.

Taken when [Colonel Robert] Abercromby's Army was at Salem ye 2nd month 1778, by the flat boatmen: 7 blankets, as good as new; 5 coverlets, three almost new; 1 bed quilt, sheets and pillowcases (I can't tell how many); 3 hats, 1 new great coat; several pairs breeches; 1 coat; a great many pairs of stockings; 2 cloth cloaks and several pairs of gloves; a new apron; a pair of stuff [sic] shoes; 5 or 6 pewter plates.[23]

The aforementioned Colonel Mawhood commanded a foraging-marauding party of approximately one thousand redcoats that crossed the river from Philadelphia and marched into Salem on March 11, 1778. The foraging for produce, grain, cattle, and horses began in earnest on the seventeenth. The plunderers met little resistance until they approached Alloways Creek, which separates Salem County into northern and southern sections. Most of the larger and more prosperous farms lay south of the creek, and the primary crossings at Quinton and at Hancock's Bridge were guarded by patriot militia. The British force, now reinforced by Major John Simcoe's Rangers, dispatched the militia guard at Quinton by luring them into an ambush on the eighteenth of March.

Then, before dawn on the twenty-first, Simcoe's Rangers paddled up Alloways Creek in flatboats, disembarked below Hancock's Bridge, and splashed their way through marshes to the patterned brick home of William Hancock, whose family name had been given to the tiny village on the south bank of the creek and to the bridge itself. After killing the sentries guarding the house, Simcoe's men entered the house from the front and rear doors. Inside sleeping were approximately twenty men of the militia and the owner of the estate. All but one of the militiamen were bayoneted and killed or mortally wounded. That one man is said to have escaped.

Also killed was the elderly William Hancock, who was asleep in his bed.[24] The massacre at Hancock's Bridge was the deadliest consequence of foraging in New Jersey during the war. However, both sides continued to take from farmers, east and west, whatever they could lay their hands on, even after the British surrender at Yorktown. Also, the trade between loyalist Dutch farmers in Bergen County and the British in New York, which had continued on a reduced scale throughout the war, became even more brisk in 1782.

Tory and refugee raids into the Hackensack Valley continued, and the illicit trade through the lines became bolder and bolder. Single farmers no longer carried a few pounds of butter or a bushel basket of vegetables into New York and brought back a sack of salt. Commercial traders openly transported country produce and salt up and down the Hackensack River at will. Whereas early in the war a farmer might drive a fat ox into New York by night and hide in the woods during the day, by 1782 farmers drove herds of cattle into the occupied city with impunity.[25]

For the duration of the American Revolution, New Jersey farmers were in a how-to survival mode: how to grow enough vegetables and fruits and raise enough animals to feed the family and, as need be, one's neighbors; how to keep the farmstead from being looted by friend and foe alike; and, finally, how to keep the fragile agricultural economy alive. After the war, most patriotic Whigs and loyalist Tories, with the exception of those loyalists who fled to Canada or to England and those farmers on both sides who couldn't forget or forgive real or imagined wrongs, got around not only to reviving the agricultural economy but revving it up a notch or two.

🦌 Fertilizing Postwar Farming

The major work to be done was to grow more vegetables, fruits and grain; raise more meat on the hoof; and grow more markets for everything New Jersey farmers could produce. The nineteenth century descendants of early Dutch, English, Scottish, Irish, Swedish, and German farmers were up to the task. First, however, they had to find a way to improve the soil. The Leni-Lenape practice of grinding in fish heads may have been enough to fertilize their relatively small gardens, but the expanding farms of the nineteenth century required something more, something that could be spread over and enrich a large tract.

Before the Revolutionary War, Benjamin Franklin, a farmer of some note but not noted as a farmer, wrote about a "bluish clay" that his hired help had discovered several inches below the surface on his property. In all probability, what Franklin's men unearthed was a claylike substance containing calcium and magnesium carbonates. At about the same time as the "bluish clay" was found in Franklin's gardens, a laborer digging a ditch on the farm of Peter Schenck near Marlboro in Monmouth County shoveled out a substance that Schenck called "marl." He spread it over a portion of his field and discovered that the vegetables grown in that area were of better quality than those raised elsewhere. His discovery attracted no particular notice, however, until 1811, when the farm was purchased by John Smock. The new owner also noticed the superior fertility of the marled field, and he shared the good news about marl with his neighbors, who then began spreading it on their fields.[26]

The same substance lay under most of the farmland in Burlington, Camden, Cumberland, Gloucester, and Salem counties, but word of the successful use of marl as a fertilizer in and around Marlboro moved south at a snail's pace. Although conclusive evidence in favor of marl existed, many farmers nevertheless were reluctant to scoop it out of the ground and sprinkle on their land. The only explanation for this delayed acceptance was a general belief among farmers, at that time, that new procedures and equipment had to prove themselves over and over before they would be adopted. It wasn't until 1826, fifteen years after the farmers in Monmouth County saw the good effects of marled fields, that Jonathan Riley down in Salem County dug up marl and made it available to other farmers.[27]

Then, as slow as farmers had been initially to catch on to the value of marl, by 1830 they were creating pits of marl and spreading it as fast as they could broadcast seed. Farmers in all of the counties where marl was present kept busy between harvest and replanting times hauling and piling the marl and then spreading it on their fields in early spring. By 1834, it was generally accepted that the use of marl had rescued or revived so much farmland and enhanced so many crops that, in the long run, some farming communities actually were saved from extinction.[28]

Reports of how marl was resuscitating so-so crops came in from all over. In the span of a single season, marginal, sandy soil in some locales was renourished to the point where the land produced quality and marketable crops. By 1849, it was claimed that some farmland in Monmouth County had increased in value by $500,000 because of the discovery and use of marl. In Salem County, the corn yield, which had amounted to fifteen or twenty bushels per acre, was increased up to sixty bushels. Marl continued to be used in large quantities until well toward the end of the nineteenth century, when it was largely replaced by commercial fertilizers.[29]

⚹ New Jersey Discovers the Tomato

At about the same time as New Jersey farmers were discovering that the clay that had been under their feet all along could enrich their fields, they also learned that the tomato, which had been cultivated in other lands for millennia, was not only safe to eat but tasted good. This latest revelation, in time, would lead to the considerable enrichment of many New Jersey farmers' bank accounts.

According to most histories of the tomato, we can thank either the Aztecs or Incas—maybe both civilizations—for first cultivating the tomato, although one Web site claims the tomato originated in the Yangtze River Valley in China. Allegedly, it was being grown in Italy in the sixteenth century (certainly long before the pizza). One fact all historians agree on is that for centuries the inhabitants of northern Europe and America thought the tomato, sometimes called the wolf peach or love apple, by any and all names was poisonous.

Legend has it that New Jersey farmers—indeed, farmers and the general populace everywhere—finally learned that *Lycopersicon esculentum* was okay to eat when, in 1820, Colonel Robert Gibbon Johnson of Salem mounted the steps of the Salem County Court House and ate either a couple of tomatoes or a bushel, depending on what version of the event you read, while a band played a funeral dirge and an audience of two thousand expected his demise at any moment. When Johnson didn't keel over, so the story goes, the people were convinced not only that the tomato could be eaten, but, if it could be eaten, it could—and should—be grown.

Whether the spectacle of 1820 ever took place, it is more reliably reported that Johnson, a historian and farmer, spent considerable time in the second decade of the nineteenth century educating other farmers and perhaps leading citizens of the time about the qualities of the tomato and its potential as a cash crop. Most importantly for the future of the Jersey tomato, he convinced farmers, particularly in southern counties, that the tomato could be grown—and in abundance—in the region's sandy soil.[30]

And grow abundantly it did! By the dawn of the twentieth century, the tomato was already one of New Jersey's most important crops. But its most spectacular development came after World War I. In 1919, the first year the state kept statistics for tomatoes, farmers planted and harvested 37,000 acres.[31]

From the beginning of the tomato's debut in New Jersey, people argued whether it should be classified as a fruit or a vegetable. Both sides made a credible case. The matter came to a head in 1883 with the passage of the Tariff Act, which imposed a duty on vegetables coming into the port of New York, but not on fruits. A businessman by the name of Nix, who imported tomatoes from the West Indies, brought suit against the New York port tax collector claiming that he (Nix) had been taxed on tomatoes as if they were vegetables when, in fact, they were fruit. Amazingly, the case wound up in the U.S. Supreme Court in 1887.

The testimony in the case consisted primarily of definitions read from dictionaries: "The plaintiff's counsel . . . read in evidence . . . the definitions of 'tomato.' The defendant's counsel then read in evidence from Webster's Dictionary the definitions of the words 'pea,' 'egg plant,' 'cucumber,' 'squash,' and 'pepper.' The plaintiff then read in evidence from Webster's and Worcester's dictionaries the definitions of 'potato,' 'turnip,' 'parsnip,' 'cauliflower,' 'cabbage,' 'carrot,' and 'bean.' No other evidence was offered by either party."

Mr. Justice Gray delivered the opinion of the court: "Botanically speaking, tomatoes are the fruit of a vine, just as cucumbers, squashes, beans and peas. But in the common language of the people, whether sellers or consumers of provisions, all these are vegetables, which are grown in kitchen gardens, and which, whether eaten cooked or raw, are, like potatoes, carrots, parsnips, turnips, beets, cauliflower, cabbage, celery and lettuce, usually served at dinner in, with or after the soup, fish or meats which constitute the principal part of the repast, and not, like fruits generally, as dessert." So be it.

✿ *Industry Advances Agriculture*
While New Jersey farmers were beginning to grow tomatoes in gardens fertilized with marl, signaling a new age for agriculture in New Jersey, the state, in the early 1800s, was racing at full speed into the Industrial Revolution. A young girl, writing more than a century later, captured this dichotomy in her exceedingly brief history of the state: "In conclusion, New Jersey is known as the Garden State. It is a good place for manufacturing."

Alexander Hamilton recognized and celebrated the dichotomy at the tail end of the eighteenth century. Unlike Thomas Jefferson and others who shared Jefferson's thinking, Hamilton did not see industrialism as a threat to agriculture. According to the most recent biography of Hamilton, by Ron Chernow, "from the outset, Hamilton emphasized that he was not scheming to replace farms with factories and that agriculture had 'intrinsically a strong claim to permanence over every other kind of industry.' Far from wishing to harm agriculture, manufacturing would create domestic markets for surplus crops. All that he recommended was that farming not have 'an exclusive predilection.'"[32]

Of course, it was Hamilton who pushed New Jersey into the Industrial Age a step or two ahead of any other state. He lent considerable support to Tench Coxe's Society for Establishing Useful Manufactures (SUM), and in April 1791 Hamilton convinced New Jersey governor William Paterson to grant SUM manufacturing monopoly status in the state and a ten-year tax exemption. In return, SUM gave the name "Paterson" to a land tract of seven hundred acres it purchased adjacent to the great falls on the Passaic River.[33]

Despite the construction of a cotton mill and a textile printing plant, SUM went bust in 1796, and Hamilton's vision of a model industrial city in New Jersey, the first anywhere in the spanking-new United States of America, seemed to fade along with SUM. However, Hamilton's plan for textile manufacturing in Paterson eventually came to fruition in the early 1800s after a system of canals provided power for not only textile mills but also for other forms of manufacturing.[34]

Hamilton's prediction that industrialism and agriculture could exist and prosper side by side also came true in New Jersey, although that is not to say that urban centers and farming communities have never infringed upon one another. They have and still do, now more than ever. However, when the populations of New Jersey's cities and those of New York and Philadelphia doubled or tripled from 1800 to 1830, largely due to the influx of immigrants working in new industries, New Jersey farms had to increase their production significantly to feed the growing masses. One observer, who was highly critical of New Jersey farmers at the end of the eighteenth century because, he claimed, they were not willing to embrace progress, had changed his mind by 1820. He credited what he conceived to be a turnaround in farmers' attitudes and accomplishments to the emergence of and opportunities presented by expanding urban markets. Of course, the observer, if he had flashed back to the middle years of the eighteenth century, he would have noted that New Jersey farmers were even then profitably marketing their produce in New York and Philadelphia.

Also, new industries that manufactured tools and equipment enabled farmers to plant and harvest more crops more efficiently. Farmers were not always quick to embrace new inventions and techniques, but once they did recognize the value of these fruits of industry, they put them to use as expeditiously as possible. For example, Charles Newbold of Burlington County nearly went broke in the 1790s trying to get his neighbors to buy and use the iron plow he had invented. His farmer friends argued that the iron plow might contaminate their land. However, Newbold suspected that their claim was merely an excuse and that the real reason for their refusing to use his invention was because they were overly cautious about experimenting with new methods and devices. The farmers' foot dragging at this point is reminiscent of the time when they were slow to accept marl as a fertilizer. In any event, a similar plow made by David Peacock of the same county caught on with farmers a decade later. Other new plows were also accepted, and, by the early decades of the nineteenth century, the majority of farmers had traded in their old wooden plows for metal ones.[35]

Industrialism and agriculture were joined in happy—if not everlasting—marriage in 1834 when the forty-four-mile Delaware & Raritan Canal connected Bordentown on the Delaware River below Trenton with New Brunswick on the Raritan River. A twenty-two-mile branch of the main canal extends north from Trenton along the Delaware River to a point nine miles south of Frenchtown in Hunterdon County. William Penn, more than 150 years earlier, had envisioned a canal being built across New Jersey to link the Delaware River (Philadelphia) and New York Bay (New York City). The Delaware & Raritan Canal nearly fulfilled his dream. Contents from barges completing the trip to New Brunswick could be off-loaded onto schooners that could then continue east on the Raritan River until the river emptied into lower New York Bay just below Staten Island.

After the Erie Canal opened in 1825, the almost-fifty-year-old America went crazy over canals. The D & R Canal was one of the first consequences of that craze; digging by Irish immigrants began in 1830. The primary reason for constructing the canal spur north from Trenton was to bring water down from a higher elevation. However, that waterway also became a link in this major new trade route for Delaware Valley farmers. Before the canal, farmers in Hunterdon, Mercer, and Somerset counties who wanted to ship their products east had to load their products onto wagons and haul them along rutted roads to Trenton, then ship them by schooner; the voyage by schooner down the bay and up the Atlantic Coast took up to two weeks. After the canal opened, farmers could transport their products to one of the hamlets that sprang up around canal locks and be relatively certain their crops would arrive in New Brunswick by mule-drawn barge in less than three days. Eventually, steam replaced mules, and as the Industrial Age continued to take hold, anthracite coal from Pennsylvania mines destined for new manufacturing plants in New Jersey became the predominant cargo aboard the barges.

While the backers of the canal were seeking approval from the New Jersey legislature, the Camden & Amboy Railroad was petitioning the government for permission to build a rail line along roughly the same route as the proposed canal. The legislature, wanting to please both parties but perhaps also being farsighted, granted permission for both projects. However, it took a number of years before the railroad moved as much cargo as the canal. The D & R Canal was followed by the Morris Canal, which linked New York and Philadelphia by connecting the Delaware and Passaic rivers. However, the D & R Canal remained the most efficient and most used of the two.[36]

As America drifted into Civil War in 1861, the federal government turned to the farmers of New Jersey to supply its armies with vegetables and fruits, and by the time Generals Lee and Grant met at Appomattox, the Garden State had become the greatest source of produce of any state in the Union.[37]

"The Biggest 🌹 CHAPTER 2
Vegetable Factory
on Earth"

When Lafayette College in Easton, Pennsylvania, closed down after the spring term of 1847, Harrison Woodhull Crosby, the college's chief gardener and assistant steward in the dining hall, went home to his farm in Jamesburg in Middlesex County, New Jersey, and scoured six little pails that his or neighbors' children perhaps once filled with sand from the seashore. He soldered lids for the cans, being careful to leave a hole in the lids, through which he then shoved stewed tomatoes. He then soldered the holes shut. Crosby was so proud of his accomplishment that the next year, in the Lafayette College kitchen, he stuffed stewed tomatoes into one thousand tin cans (not sand pails) and sent samples to such notables as President Polk, Queen Victoria, New Jersey lawmakers, and Horace Greeley at the *New York Tribune*.[1]

The samples were an immediate hit, and commercial canning of tomatoes in New Jersey and perhaps in America was born. As the new food processing industry used the term, canning meant packing vegetables, fruits, and condiments in bottles as well as tin cans.

Crosby's new business made headlines. More importantly, news of what he had done spread from farmer to farmer and from farmers to their wives, and before very long mom-and-pop can houses popped up on the New Jersey landscape like dandelions in springtime. The small-time, small-town can houses eventually were replaced by big-time, big-world food processors—those who canned, bottled, and froze—and they would pretty much dictate what New Jersey farms would grow for the next one hundred years and what the world would eat.

What farmers grew most for a very long while was the tomato, the fruit that became a vegetable that became not only edible but downright tasty and, finally, became a favorite of canners and consumers. The tomato was canned whole, stewed, pureed, as juice and, later, in soup—very famous soup. Whereas a visitor to New Jersey in the first decade of the nineteenth century would have been hard pressed to find a tomato garden of any size in all of the state, by the later decades the visitor would likely not pass a farm that did not include acres of tomatoes.

As always, of course, the farmer had to gamble that what he sowed he could reap, and what he reaped would bring a profit, at least sufficient to enable him to maintain his family, and with enough money left over to buy seed for next year's crop.

In 1888, the *Salem Standard and Jerseyman* estimated the net profit a farmer might realize on his two-dollar investment in a pound of tomato seed. The newspaper figured that the cost of preparing and plowing a five-acre seedbed, cultivating and fertilizing it, purchasing baskets, and, finally, picking and delivering fifty tons of tomatoes to the can house would amount to $183.10. If the farmer sold his fifty tons of tomatoes at six dollars per ton, he would realize $300 in gross profit. His net profit would be $116.90. The newspaper speculated that, if bad weather or other adverse conditions should cause the farmer's five acres to produce only thirty tons of tomatoes instead of fifty, the net profit would be reduced to $41.90.

Regardless of the profit he might realize, the farmer was still obliged to take his tomatoes to the can house. For many farmers, the trip from farm to processor began in the evening when the tomatoes picked that day were loaded into baskets and the baskets then piled onto the horse drawn wagon. The farmer would travel most of the night, arriving at the can house early in the morning.[2] In many ways, as we will note later, this ordeal did not change greatly after the advent of the combustion engine.

🌟 Canneries Multiply

The small can house that received the wagonloads of tomatoes was, in the early days of food processing, a fairly primitive business. A block-and-tackle lowered and raised crates of canned tomatoes in and out of large boilers heated by wood that had been cut from a nearby forest. Water for the boilers usually was piped by gravity from a lake or stream; sometimes, however, water had to be brought to the can house by wagon. The entire operation was hard work.[3]

One of the earliest canneries was located at the North American Phalanx in Monmouth County. The North American Phalanx was a cooperative commune based on the social and economic theories of François Marie Charles Fourier of France. The commune was established on 673 acres in 1843 and continued to 1855; during that period, the population fluctuated between 125 and 150 adults and children. Men and women worked at jobs that suited their natural abilities and fulfilled the needs of the commune. Among the tasks was working in the commune's cannery.[4]

When the commune dissolved in 1855 because of philosophical differences and financial problems, one of its founders, John Bucklin, purchased at auction eighty-six acres of Phalanx farmland and the cannery. In 1862, his son Charles became a partner, and the cannery name was changed to J & C. S. Bucklin Company. By the end of the century, Charles's ingenuity not only had caused the family business to prosper, but his inventions also were instrumental in modernizing the canning business in New Jersey and elsewhere. Toward the end of his life, he recalled those days when he and the canning industry were shifting into high gear:

> In 1873, I built and patented a foot power filler. It was the first filling machine put on the market. . . . In 1887, I built and patented the Cyclone Pulp Machine and soon after a Gang Tomato Filler, filling six cans at a time. In 1902, I erected a canning factory in

Pennington, N.J. for the Pennington Canning Company and built a continuous steam cooker, which I patented. . . . . About 1907, I was interested in a coating for the inside of cans and built a machine for applying the coating to a made can and also for coating the caps. Both machines were patented and assigned to the American Can Company.[5]

By the end of the nineteenth century, the food processing industry, which bottled and canned fruits and condiments as well as tomatoes, was booming throughout New Jersey. In the north, the Paterson Preserving Company boasted that "connoisseurs pronounce [our] sauces, pickles and other goods . . . equal to those from the world-famous Crosse and Blackwell English establishment"; the neighboring Passaic Pickle Works provided lively competition. Some of the many other establishments included the Hightstown Cannery Factories in Mercer County, Egg Harbor City Cannery in Atlantic County, J. H. Butterfoss in Hunterdon County, Philadelphia Pickling Company in Cape May, and Hannan Brothers Cannery in Cumberland County.

David and James Hannan bought into the canning business big-time in 1888, planting every one of their one hundred-plus acres in tomatoes. They built their cannery behind the family home on Deerfield Street in Deerfield. It wasn't pretty, but it was efficient: a 120-foot-long, unpainted frame building, with a brick chimney and water tank plunked in the middle. On days when canning began early in the morning and continued past dark, farmers perched on their wagons laden with tomatoes, waited, and watched for a puff of black smoke from the brick chimney that indicated the boilers were being fired. A blast from the plant whistle was the signal to the farmers to begin lining up at the plant's unloading dock.[6]

On their way to becoming stewed, the tomatoes were first placed in containers and dunked in boiling water. From there, they were transported to women peelers, who stripped them of their skin and placed the now-bare tomatoes in one bucket and the skins in another. No part of the tomato went unused. The waste trimmed from the tomatoes was collected and later sold to individuals or small companies that fermented the material in large vats and eventually turned it into tomato paste that was marketed in Philadelphia and New York.[7]

The Hannan brothers' business struggled to survive in the infant years of its existence, but then it took off, increasing its employees from eighteen to sixty. In the first decade of the twentieth century, the brothers sold a quarter million and more cans of their Deerfield Brand Hand Picked Tomatoes, most of them to the Great Atlantic & Pacific Tea Company (A & P).[8]

Then there was the Brower Sisters' Kitchen of Point Pleasant, which, at the time, was unique in two ways: (1) the Kitchen canned, mostly in glass bottles, just about anything and everything a New Jersey farmer could grow, and (2) the Brower Sisters were actually husband and wife. The Kitchen's fifteen skilled women began each year canning asparagus in the spring, followed by a succession of tomatoes and other vegetables and fruits; the year concluded when the Kitchen bottled syrups, relishes, jams, and jellies. The only explanation for the name of the company is that Trevone Height Brower and his wife, Mabel, liked it.

Nearly all the fruits and vegetables canned by the Browers were grown in Monmouth County. The exception was white cherries, which they imported from western states. Workers packed quart jars, jelly glasses, and jam jars in wooden boxes that were sold directly to customers throughout the nation. None were sold through stores or brokers. Mr. Brower died in 1923, but Mrs. Brower was still running the Kitchen as late as the 1940s.[9]

Perhaps foretelling the future of food processing, when a single, large company would own and operate plants throughout the country, some small but enterprising canners in the nineteenth century ran two or more plants at the same time. Fogg & Ayres and Luke Smith each had three plants going at the same time in Salem County. Smith's can houses were in Alloway, Elmer, and Claysville, now a neighborhood outside Salem City, and he made the rounds of each plant every day. The local train schedule made it possible. Smith boarded a train in Salem City at 6:30 in the morning and got off at Alloway Junction. While he visited his plant there, the train went on to Quinton. On its way back from Quinton, the same train picked up Smith and dropped him off in Elmer. Upon completion of his business in Elmer, Smith boarded another train, which took him to Claysville.[10]

Cannery employees worked long hours for little pay in high heat generated by the process that peeled and stewed tomatoes. The boy Wade Ewen worked for Smith in the Alloway plant, pushing tin cans down a chute from the second floor where they were stockpiled to the canning floor below. One day Ewen and several other boys who worked for Smith decided they would strike for a raise of two cents, to ten cents an hour. Of course, no union existed to support their request, and even their parents didn't back them. Wade's father, the respected family doctor, Warren Ewen, told his son that either he could forget asking for a raise or face a woodshed thrashing. Young Wade and his friends and coworkers gave up.[11]

Not only were the small canneries overheated to the extreme, but their employees, most of whom were women, worked under very unhealthy conditions. The Hannan Brothers operation was typical. Very little thought was given to sanitation. The plant had no screens, and the doors were always kept open to admit a breeze, if there was one, and to allow the steam generated by the boilers to, it was hoped, drift out. Workers regularly washed down the floors, worktables, and wooden pails, but nothing was sterilized. Tomato juice and other effluent dribbled down an open gutter in the cannery that led outside and eventually into a dry streambed, where it became a foul-smelling, bubbling pond.[12]

By the beginning of the twentieth century, hard-working, long-suffering women could earn as much as ten dollars for a week of toil. Typically, a worker could keep track of her earnings by counting up the number of small, brass disks that were dropped by the plant foreman into the bottom of each sixteen-quart wooden pail before it was filled with scalded tomatoes. Each token was worth four cents. When the worker had accumulated fifty such disks, she could exchange them for a larger token worth two dollars. Five of those tokens equaled the ten dollars. To earn those ten dollars, the worker had to have processed four thousand quarts of hot tomatoes.[13]

Late in the nineteenth century, F. E. Daniels, a chemist, worked up a table showing what typically happened to a hundred tons of tomatoes in the canning process. Fifty tons wound up in cans, according to Daniels. Of the remaining fifty tons, slightly more than forty-four tons consisted of skins and cuttings. Of that quantity, thirty-nine tons of pulp and juice often were sold as a mix called Cyclone Liquor (perhaps named after Charles Bucklin's Cyclone Pulp Machine). The Pure Food Law of 1906, however, ended the sale of Cyclone Liquor because it was easily contaminated.[14]

The twentieth century boom in the Garden State, as we have already noted, was already making noise in the last half of the nineteenth century, and most of it was heard coming from the Anderson and Campbell cannery in Camden on Second Street between Market and Arch streets. The partners, Abraham Anderson and Joseph Campbell, joined forces in 1870 or 1871. The company promoted to wide acclaim its Celebrated Beefsteak Tomato—only one to a can—and Anderson's Celebrated Mince Meat. The firm also gained notoriety for being the first cannery in the United States to pack fancy small peas.[15]

The Anderson-Campbell partnership didn't last very long, and by 1873 Campbell was operating the cannery himself under the trade name of Joseph Campbell Preserve Company. In 1882, however, Campbell badly needed investment capital to expand the business, and he turned to Arthur Dorrance, a man of money from Bristol, Pennsylvania. The expansion financed in large part by new partner Dorrance allowed the company to market preserves, jellies, prepared meats, sauces, canned fruits, vegetables, and "goods of all sorts and description."[16] One of those most important goods was ready-to-serve beefsteak tomato soup.

The Joseph Campbell Preserve Company, the New Jersey tomato, and the farmers who grew the tomatoes owed much of their twentieth-century fame and fortune to a decision made reluctantly by Arthur Dorrance in 1897. Dorrance, who had acquired the controlling interest in the company, is reported to have had some misgivings about hiring his twenty-four-year-old nephew, John. The young man had just earned a doctorate in organic chemistry in Germany after earning degrees in chemical engineering from the Massachusetts Institute of Technology. The uncle thought his nephew was, in the words of today's management when it declines to hire too-bright aspirants, overly qualified. The old man gave in, however, and took on Dr. Dorrance as a chemist he thought the company didn't need. His salary was set at $7.50 a week, and he was expected to stick to the laboratory and not get in the way of real business.

🌺 Condensed Soup Invented

Get in the way? He *showed* the way, and it ultimately led to a bright future and riches for the company and, not incidentally, for New Jersey farmers. Not very long after being hired, Dr. Dorrance emerged from his modest laboratory one day and declared that he had invented condensed soup. He had found a way to remove the water from a can of Campbell's soup, thereby reducing the volume of a can from thirty-two ounces to approximately ten ounces. Even more importantly, the discovery allowed the company to sell a can of soup for a dime instead of thirty-four cents. The five varieties of soup then being canned—tomato, consommé, vegetable, chicken, and oxtail—became instantly popular. Tomato soup, one hundred eight years later, is still ranked among the top ten selling dry grocery items in America's supermarkets.

The year after he came out of the laboratory with condensed soup, in 1898, John's uncle Arthur increased his nephew's weekly salary by a dollar and a half to nine dollars. One might argue persuasively that a 20 percent increase in salary was hardly enough to show the company's gratitude to Dr. Dorrance for making it exceedingly wealthy in the upcoming century. Whether Dr. Dorrance felt his laboratory wizardry had been unappreciated and he had not been fairly compensated, no one knows. In any event, he did stay out of the lab at least long enough to launch a turn-of-the-century advertising campaign featuring his discovery. He promoted his condensed soup by plastering New York City streetcars with broadsides featuring a red and white can bearing the label "Campbell's Soup." However, those two words, now easily recognized around the world, did not become an official part of the company name until 1922.

Shortly after the Joseph Campbell Preserve Company across the Delaware River from Philadelphia concluded that condensed soup was going to be exceedingly more popular with consumers than its beefsteak tomato soup and canned mincemeat, Henry John Heinz opened his first New Jersey plant downriver in Salem in the hope his Pittsburgh-based company might turn a profit by bottling puree made from Jersey tomatoes. Like Joseph Campbell and other men of gigantic ideas and extraordinary perseverance who were born and raised in the nineteenth century and indelibly stamped their name on the twentieth, Heinz early on discovered that hard work was unending but that success sometimes came in spurts that could rattle even the most sturdy constitution.

At age sixteen, in 1860, Heinz managed a garden—not really a farm by any standard—in which he grew primarily horseradish, then much in demand by Pittsburgh families. He and a workforce of three or four women ground the horseradish, bottled it, and sold it to local grocers. E. D. McCafferty, who at one time was Heinz's private secretary, credits this modest horseradish business as "the germ from which the business of the H. J. Heinz Company as a packer of food products developed."[17]

However, before the H. J. Heinz Company was conceived, Heinz, at age twenty-five, partnered with another up-and-coming food processor, L. C. Noble, to create Heinz, Noble and Company. Their intention was to bottle and sell horseradish, pickles, sauerkraut, and vinegar to more and more customers, and the business opened in a two-story farmhouse on the northern edge of the city. Within five years, the company moved into larger quarters. At the time, Heinz, Noble and Company's assets included one hundred acres of vegetable and herb gardens, twenty-four horses, a dozen wagons and a vinegar factory.[18]

Like many other businesses of the time and since, Heinz, Noble and Company expanded too quickly, and, in the banking panic of 1875, the partners found themselves in severe financial straits. When the grocers who were their customers refused to extend credit, the company declared bankruptcy. Heinz, married with two children and living in a grand house, was virtually penniless.

Undaunted, and with little choice but to attempt a new beginning, Heinz joined with his brother John and cousin Frederick to start a new business. The panic that closed down Heinz, Noble and Company was still forcing even established companies out of business, but the three men persisted and survived 1875. Although a

very tough year financially, it was a stellar year for product introduction: tomato ketchup. Other products followed: red and green
pepper sauce, cider vinegar, apple butter, chili sauce, mincemeat,
mustard, tomato soup, olives, pickled onions, pickled cauliflower,
baked beans and the first sweet pickles ever brought to market.[19]

❦ Heinz Bottles Ketchup

Ketchup (almost never referred to any longer as catsup) originated
several centuries ago in the Far East, but the Asian version—
spelled kechap or ke-tsiap—generally featured a fish brine base.
Later variations included oysters, mushrooms, and shallots. For
a while, the only common ingredient in ketchups was vinegar.
Although tomato ketchups of one kind or another were around
before Heinz came out with his brand, the Heinz ketchup soon became number one with homemakers. Of course, ketchup bearing
any label is still considered the most popular condiment in the
United States, although salsa is now a strong runner-up.

One day in 1896, Heinz boarded the elevated railroad in New
York City to take him to a business appointment. Like any out-of-
towner, Heinz looked out the car window and marveled at the
spectacular sights of the bustling city. As he was nearing his stop,
he spotted a sign that advertised twenty-one styles of shoes. Mc-
Cafferty quoted his one-time boss describing what happened next:
"I said to myself, 'We do not have styles of products, but we do
have varieties of products. Counting up how many we had, I
counted well beyond fifty-seven, but fifty-seven kept coming back
into my mind. I got off the train, immediately went down to the
lithographer's, where I designed a streetcar card [proclaiming
Heinz's fifty-seven varieties] and had it distributed throughout the
United States. I myself did not realize how highly successful a slogan it was going to be."[20]

A market for fresh tomatoes and other vegetables and fruits
has always existed—and still does, of course—but as the new century dawned, more farmers sold more tomatoes to more canneries
for more money. By 1900, can house prices were better, and most
South Jersey growers keyed themselves to the tin men, though
only a man with seeds in his head completely ignored the fresh

market. About fifty New Jersey canneries bought tomatoes in 1902, particularly in Cumberland, Salem, and Burlington counties. The State Board of Agriculture reported that in 1902 tomatoes were grown statewide, but only the region south of a line between Trenton and New Brunswick had commercial importance.

The Heinz plant in Salem opened in 1906, the year H.J. celebrated his sixty-second birthday, and the plant's first two years of operation were devoted almost exclusively to the bottling of tomato puree. By 1909, the company employed three hundred persons and decided to process its prized ketchup. Although Heinz did not boast a John Dorrance in its research lab, the Salem plant nevertheless conducted experiments that improved the texture, flavor, color, and juice quality of its prized Aristocrat Tomato.

In the first decade of the twentieth century, the Joseph Campbell Company, H. J. Heinz, and other canneries purchased most of their Jersey tomatoes on the open market. Before 1912, for example, only seven hundred acres of tomatoes were grown exclusively for and under the control of the Joseph Campbell Company. Tomatoes harvested on thousands of other acres varied greatly in overall quality. In that year, Campbell's appointed Harry F. Hall as manager of farming operations. He was charged with the responsibility for creating uniform standards that would ensure that farmers grew better-quality tomatoes under contract to the Joseph Campbell Company. He became widely known and respected among New Jersey tomato growers for helping them to improve the soil and use a better quality of tomato seed. He also advocated planting seed in hotbeds and cold frames to increase the length of season. At harvest time, he urged farmers to be extra careful to pick and pack only ripe tomatoes. His advice helped to guarantee that farmers would be paid the highest price for their crops by canneries.[21]

Through Hall, the Joseph Campbell Company made contact with R. Vincent Crine, a successful farmer in Monmouth County, who had concluded that New Jersey tomato farmers could get a head start in the spring if they put into the ground plants grown in a warmer clime during January and February. By 1918, young tomato plants grown in South Carolina were being exported to New Jersey farmers; in the following year, Crine moved to Georgia and continued to ship plants north after the ground thawed.[22]

Just as the tomato itself was being perfected, so was the process for putting it into bottles and cans, and as the number of farmers growing tomatoes increased, so did the number of manufacturers of tin cans and glass bottles. Newark and Passaic each boasted two tin can manufacturers, and Cumberland Glass Company in Bridgeton and Salem Glass Works were among those companies supplying bottles. The tin can used in the early decades of the twentieth century was a considerable improvement over the cans Harrison W. Crosby used to send his stewed tomatoes to celebrities in 1847.

When Crosby was messing around with commercial canning in the Lafayette College kitchen, one man could produce only ten cans a day by cutting out the rectangular bodies and round ends, shaping the can around a cylinder, and then carefully soldering the body and the ends together. Each can had a hole in the top where the tomato product would be inserted. After the can was filled, a cap was soldered into position. Although later equipment speeded up the process considerably, the cap and hole design continued to be used for almost one hundred years.[23]

By the time the Joseph Campbell Company was gearing up for its first run of condensed soups, the tin can of Crosby's era had been replaced by the open-top can. This enabled the can to be filled more easily and faster, and neither the top nor bottom of the can had to be soldered, because the ends were crimped by a machine that tightly sealed the can. In 1910, a manufacturer could produce thirty-five thousand tin cans a day.[24] Despite Campbell's success with canned soups, other tomato products including ketchup, puree, and chutney that were still sold in glass by other processors remained popular because the early twentieth century housewife was long accustomed to glass containers. After all, she had preserved foods in glass in her own kitchen for decades. Plus, when she went to the market, she could see what she was buying in a glass container; furthermore, a bottle can be reused.

🍅 Ritter Joins Campbell and Heinz

On May 16, 1916, as war raged in Europe, the P. J. Ritter Company of Philadelphia purchased land on the bank of the Cohansey River in Bridgeton, Cumberland County, that had once been the site of a

Leni-Lenape village (for years after, employees dug up arrowheads). William H. Ritter, who had assumed active management of the company in 1902 when the business was producing ketchup—the company called it catsup—on a Henry Ford-like assembly line, was looking forward to locating his processing plant in the heart of the Garden State's tomato country. However, he was immediately faced with a monumental problem. The company had the land but not a processing plant; it needed to build one, but the war overseas had created a shortage of building materials. Not about to be closed down before he opened, Ritter purchased the old Convention Hall in Philadelphia at Broad Street and Allegheny Avenue and had it shipped piece by piece to the Bridgeton site. Canning operations began in August of the following year, 1917.[25] The Big Two of canning in New Jersey became the Big Three: Campbell, Heinz, and Ritter.

The Cohansey River served two purposes for the Ritter processing plant. While Bridgeton was in the heart of tomato country, the plant also purchased tomatoes from Delaware and Maryland. Farmers in lower Maryland, in particular, ordinarily harvested tomatoes before farmers in southern New Jersey. Tomatoes from these two states usually were shipped to Ritter by boat and barge. In the case of boats, where baskets of tomatoes were located in the hold, off-loading was super-hard work. Men spent most of their time bent over, and high heat and mosquitoes both took their toll. Horse-drawn wagons transported the baskets of tomatoes from the boat and barge to a loading platform at the plant, where they were emptied into a trough. The river also served as a handy depository for wastewater from the processing plant. It was not uncommon for boys who swam in the river to emerge covered with tomato skins. Many youths recalled emerging from a swim in the river with tomato skins covering them from head to toe.[26]

At the end of 1917, the first year of operations in Bridgeton and the year when American soldiers first saw combat in World War I, the Ritter ledger showed a net profit that exceeded the previous year's figure by nearly $1.8 million. The company attributed its very good year to two factors: the decision to establish a processing plant in Bridgeton, and the new demand placed upon all processors to supply foodstuffs to American servicemen overseas and in stateside training camps.[27]

The year 1918 presented an unusual dilemma. While the U.S. Army's demand for Ritter products remained great, the company had trouble supplying the army's needs because an overly bountiful tomato crop came in early and so quickly that Ritter couldn't process the tomatoes fast enough. At one point, as many as two hundred wagons loaded with tomatoes stood in line on Glass Street waiting to be unloaded. Eventually, much of that year's crop had to be returned to the farms as fertilizer. The tomato glut, however, caused Ritter to consider expanding its plant and operations to accommodate the prodigious production generated by farmers of the Garden State. Over the next ten years, therefore, Ritter closed five other plants on the East Coast and concentrated all its efforts on adding to and improving its Bridgeton facilities. These included a new warehouse and a manufacturing plant capable of processing eight thousand to ten thousand baskets of tomatoes per day; soon, that number was doubled. By 1929, the Bridgeton plant was turning out each day twelve thousand cases of catsup, four thousand cases of pork and beans, and three thousand five-gallon cans of tomato puree. In addition, Ritter's field men helped farmers stretch the normal harvest into two summer months instead of one, thereby helping to head off another glut.[28]

Although the Big Three food processors and most of the large tomato farms were located in South Jersey, smaller canneries and farms were still scattered throughout the Garden State. In the first two decades of the twentieth century, farms of all sizes were planted with tomatoes of all varieties and harvested in the summer; some, naturally, made better end products than others. The stage was set for someone to come along and develop the one tomato that would end up becoming the best juice, ketchup, puree or soup. Enter Professor Lyman G. Schermerhorn of the New Jersey Agricultural Experiment Station.

The Experiment Station had its roots planted in 1864 when the Rutgers Board of Trustees purchased a run-down farm of almost one hundred acres on the cheap and designated it for experimental and practical instruction. The first practical step was to make the farm productive. At the time of purchase, the trustees' bargain was in very deplorable condition. The soil was so poor that a crop of wheat planted in 1864 averaged only six bushels an acre; other acreage yielded mostly hay that was so filled with weeds that it could not be sold. By the latter decades of the nineteenth century, the fertility of the soil had been restored and Rutgers could focus on research. The farm officially became the Experiment Station in 1880, and its new charge was to hire competent chemists who could expertly analyze soils, fertilizers, and other materials and processes related to agriculture.[29]

✷ Behold, the Rutgers Tomato

Professor Schermerhorn joined the station staff in 1914 as a specialist in vegetable studies. By the end of the next decade his studies were focused on the tomato, and in 1929 he and his colleagues babied into existence a tomato that had all the promise of becoming *the* tomato. However, the research team continued its experiments until, five years later, it produced four descendants of the 1929 variety. They numbered them 444, 490, 497, and 500. Professor Schermerhorn then selected seventy-five farmers located throughout the state to grow the four Rutgers-bred selections. Five years later, in September 1934, Professor Schermerhorn decided that No. 500 had fared the best of the four varieties, and he crowned it the Rutgers tomato. Most tomato experts still believe that No. 500 was the best tomato ever grown in the Garden State or anywhere else. For the remainder of the twentieth century, the Rutgers tomato was the preferred choice of 75 percent of commercial growers in the United States.[30]

Professor Schermerhorn had even more laurels to earn. He and his staff of researchers set to work coming up with a tomato variety that would be especially appealing to shoppers at roadside stands and supermarkets. They wanted to develop a tomato that was smooth, of high quality, which ripened ahead of the average tomato, and could sit on the shelf a while without losing texture or good taste. The result from this ongoing research was the Queens tomato. It became popular with consumers as soon as it was displayed on roadside stands. One farmer, who initially planted one hundred Queens plants on his eighty-five-acre farm, couldn't pick enough tomatoes to satisfy customer demand. So, the next year he put in 3,500 plants, and the year after that 8,000, and the third year he put in 36,000 plants.[31]

Professor Schermerhorn became something of a broadcast celebrity in the 1940s and 1950s, appearing as a frequent guest on at least two network radio programs. Ingrid Nelson Waller, who apparently interviewed Professor Schermerhorn for her 1955 book, reported that he took "the story of New Jersey's super vegetables into the homes of farmer and layman from Bar Harbor to Miami, from Cape Cod to Hollywood. He admits, however, that to him it is the Rutgers tomato that will always be something special. 'I would have been content,' he comments, 'just to have bred a tomato like Rutgers.'"[32]

There was Professor Schermerhorn talking up Jersey tomatoes on radio, Garden State farmers growing them like gangbusters, canners processing them in overtime mode, and markets overflowing with ripe tomatoes and every product made from them. And Ed McNemar couldn't have been happier—or busier.

McNemar, who died at age eighty-two in 2005, was one of dozens of men and perhaps some women who transported tomatoes from farms to processors in New Jersey, Delaware, and Maryland all day and all night during the late summers of the 1940s and 1950s—prime time for the Jersey tomato. Months before his death, he recalled one occasion when he hauled tomatoes nonstop to processors in all three states; he was loading up, driving, and unloading for twenty hours straight, with only an occasional nap while he was waiting in line to have the baskets piled high in his ten-wheeler emptied of tomatoes. Ordinarily, the truck contained one thousand baskets, each basket holding thirty-five pounds of tomatoes.

"I most often carried tomatoes destined for the open market," McNemar recalled. That meant that his laden baskets went to whichever processor would give the farmer the best price. On the other hand, farmers under contract to a processor were paid whatever they and the processor had agreed to in advance, which often was less than what the farmer could earn on the open market. Consequently, said McNemar, some farmers sold the larger share of their crop to the processor to whom they were under contract, but kept out a share to sell on the open market. Of course, farmers who did this were not abiding strictly to their contract, said McNemar, but "everybody knew what was going on and mostly looked the other way." In cases where the contract farmer was also selling on the open market, he added, the farmer might arrange for the truck to come by after dark to pick up the part of his harvest headed for the open market.

Truckers could spend the better part of a day or night standing in line at a cannery waiting for their tomatoes to be offloaded. "I've been in lines that were, literally, miles long," McNemar said. It was not unusual for trucks to be stretched up and down most of the streets of East Camden waiting their turn at one of two Campbell Soup Company plants. "If they shut the gates at night before you got in, you had the choice of coming back in the morning and getting at the end of the line or staying put and sleeping in the cab of your truck." McNemar remembered a time when his wife-to-be accompanied him on a run to Campbell Soup. "They closed the gates before I could unload my tomatoes. I didn't want Doris to spend the night with me in the cab, so I put her on a bus for Salem and home."

When the same long lines included both trucks whose tomatoes came from a contract farmer and trucks hauling tomatoes being sold on the open market, McNemar said, the cannery usually would unload the contract farmers' trucks first. On occasions when the crop was beyond bumper and the processor couldn't handle all the tomatoes in all the trucks, those vehicles carrying open market tomatoes might stand in line for days until their tomatoes turned to mush. In such cases, the drivers would take their baskets back to the farmers and the mush would become fertilizer.

McNemar said he had no wish to forget nor does he resent those long-ago days and nights of driving, driving, driving, and standing in lines that snaked through blistering city streets or along dusty country roads. After all, he played a central role in those heady days when the Jersey tomato was the king—or queen—of vegetables and prized from coast to coast and beyond. Instead of dwelling on the frustration and monotony that were his constant companions in the cab of his truck, McNemar's memory recalled an early morning when he was—what else—in line before a cannery in Baltimore. He had spent the night there, and at six o'clock in the morning his feet were still hanging out the window. He was awakened by a young voice, "Mister, can I have a tomato?" McNemar looked out and saw the upturned face of a boy. "Sure, you can have a tomato." The boy disappeared. "The next time I saw the kid he was pulling a large wagon filled to overflowing with tomatoes. I think he took the wagon down the street and sold the tomatoes somewhere. That was okay by me; I didn't care."

In 1945, as World War II ended and Ed McNemar was hauling tomatoes night and day to this cannery and that one, 45,000 acres of the Garden State were planted in tomatoes. Eighty percent of those tomatoes were sold to canneries under contract. The crop in that year was valued at $10 million, which was twice the valuation of all vegetables, including tomatoes, in 1900.[33]

That same year, Jim Sclafani was honorably discharged from the United States Army and sent home to Brooklyn, where his immigrant parents and their sons had been processing and distributing foodstuffs to primarily Italian American families since the late 1800s. However, he had almost no time to enjoy his homecoming. Sclafani learned his family, which had expanded its business over the decades out of a little store on Elizabeth Street by "following the railroad tracks west to St. Louis and south to Miami," had just purchased the Violet Packing Company (named for the state flower), a tomato processing plant in Williamstown, Gloucester County, and decided that he and brother Melvin would manage the business.

At the time, Violet Packing Company was dwarfed by such giant food processors as Campbell Soup Company and P. J. Ritter. John V. Sharp, who first canned tomatoes out of a shed in his backyard, started the business in 1882 at 123 Railroad Avenue in Williamstown (part of Monroe Township). Although the operation was no more sophisticated than most other processors, as each workday began Sharp required his employees to place their right hand on a Bible and swear they would not reveal any secrets about the business.

Sclafani reminisced about the day he and his brother came to Williamstown to manage the Violet Packing Company: "When we took over in 1945, [the company] had two coal-fired, 100-horse-powered boilers. Coal came in by railroad coal cars and was transported either by the company dump truck or [by wheelbarrow] to the boiler room at the rear of the plant." The man in charge of "cooking" the tomatoes was John Sutton. "I very clearly remember his old methods of determining the finishing point of the first batch of pizza sauce. . . . He took an old wooden board about two inches wide and twenty-four inches long. I asked him, 'John, what gives?' He replied, 'This is how I determine the finishing point of ketchup, by putting sauce on the stick and [figuring] the time of flow.'"

That first batch of pizza sauce in 1946 was the first ever made in New Jersey and, the family is proud to say, only the second in the nation. The recipe for the sauce was concocted by James's brother Dominick, and the sauce was marketed under the Don Pepino label and sold to restaurants, institutions, and supermarkets. In 1986, a newspaper reporter read the label on a can of the sauce: "Made from whole tomatoes, corn oil, seasoned with salt and spices . . . Special Formula." What *is* the Special Formula—the recipe—the reporter wanted to know. He quoted Sclafani's reply, "It's so simple, it's pathetic; that's what makes it right." But he never divulged it. Today, Violet Packing Company has a well-scrubbed, technologically advanced testing lab where its products are analyzed in various ways. When, however, I asked a technician how the lab tests the pizza sauce, the response was as simple as the recipe, "We use a spoon. If it doesn't taste good, all the other tests don't matter."

Not only did Violet Packing pioneer pizza sauce, it also was the first cannery to transport tomatoes in bulk rather than in baskets. Sclafani attended a 1959 conference in Atlantic City where a professor from the University of Maryland recommended the new means of transportation. Upon his return, Sclafani first met some resistance from growers, but he finally convinced them that hauling tomatoes in dump trucks was the better way.

The bulk processing began with the tomatoes being dumped directly from the truck into a flume leading into the plant. Then they went through a washer, down an inspection line, and into a pulping machine. The next step was a one-thousand-gallon surge tank that led to the cooker. When the tomatoes were done in the cooker, the tank was emptied and oils and seasonings were added. Supervisors sampled the product throughout the process.[34]

An almost-forgotten attic room in the Violet Packing Company plant contains processing equipment from the company's early days that was invented or perfected by Sharp, the founder, and his successor, George Pfeiffer. It was Pfeiffer, in the first two decades of the twentieth century, who designed equipment powered by a foot treadle that included a tomato crusher and a device that first filled No. 10 cans with sauce and then inserted the cans into wooden shipping crates. Jim Sclafani, something of an innovator himself, said of Pfeifer, "He was a genius."

✿ Seabrook Pioneers Frozen Food

Another Garden State food-processing innovator of the twentieth century who deserved the genius label was Charles F. Seabrook (called simply C.F. by everyone except his wife). However, while Campbell, Heinz, Ritter, Sclafani, and other canneries were profiting from 45,000 acres of Jersey tomatoes in the middle of the century, Seabrook Farms in Upper Deerfield, Cumberland County, was making money from an equal number of acres planted in nearly every vegetable *other* than the tomato. Under a headline that read "Biggest Vegetable Factory on Earth," *Life Magazine*, in 1955, called Seabrook Farms "the biggest, best-organized vegetable factory in the world. Here, with the mass production adeptness usually associated with motor cars, Seabrook Farms last year grew, gathered and froze one hundred million pounds of twenty-nine vegetables and fruits. Its packaged output of lima beans would have stretched 2,250 miles. Its production of asparagus equaled one serving for every resident of New York, Florida, Washington and Texas. In size and degree of integration, Seabrook stands unique, even in a time when U.S. farms generally are growing larger, fewer and more mechanized."[35]

Seabrook Farms was unique all right. It had a lock on three firsts. It was the first true agribusiness in America. None other than B. C. Forbes, founder of the leading business publication *Forbes Magazine*, referred to C.F. as the "Henry Ford of Agriculture," and, as previously noted, *Life Magazine* compared the company's food processing line to a car assembly line. C.F. was an exceptional, successful, and completely self-taught construction engineer. Almost single-handedly, he designed and supervised the construction of Seabrook Farms' food processing and storage facilities, employee housing, garages and shops, and even two railroad spurs. John Cunningham could write in 1955, "No vegetable enterprise in the United States is bigger than Seabrook Farms [and] no farm in the nation is more highly mechanized."[36]

Seabrook Farms was the first company anywhere in the world to produce frozen vegetables on a large scale. Belford, C.F.'s eldest son, spent the summer after his freshman year at Princeton in the Massachusetts laboratory of Clarence Birdseye. The following year, 1930, using ammonia from a crude freezer, Belford quick-froze 20,000 pounds of lima beans. That was just the beginning. C.F. went to the New York City headquarters of General Foods, which had purchased the patented Birdseye process, and suggested a partnership. Birdseye and Seabrook were a perfect match. General Foods had patents, capital, and marketing know-how, and Seabrook Farms knew how to grow new varieties of vegetables that were suitable for freezing.[37]

Seabrook Farms created the first rural global village of its kind in the United States. The huge workforce (close to seven thousand in season at midpoint of the twentieth century) consisted of men and women representing twenty-five nationalities or cultures. They included men who had fought for the White Russians against Bolshevism; Italian immigrant families; hundreds of men from the West Indies; twenty-five hundred Japanese Americans direct from World War II internment camps; Estonians, Latvians, Lithuanians, Ukrainians, Germans, and other Europeans from refugee camps; out-of-work men and their families from Appalachia; many African American college girls, who were flown north by Seabrook in a converted army transport to work summers on the food assembly lines; and others. They lived in housing built by the company; they frequented a community center built by the company; their youngest children went to a day-care facility created by the company (again, one of the first such enterprises sponsored by a business for its employees); and their older children attended a K–8 school largely designed and financed by C.F. Linda Keerdoja, who came with her parents from Estonia in 1949, took a moment in 1995 to reminisce about the global village: "What started out as strange and different had in time become normal and natural. Our ethnic and cultural differences did not disappear, but neither were they a barrier to our getting along. Multiculturalism, a popular buzzword of the 1990s, is not a new concept. In Seabrook more than forty years ago, it was already a fact of everyday life."[38]

Seabrook Farms began producing frozen vegetables and, later, frozen dinners and other specialty dishes under its own name in 1943, and the company became the major provider to U.S. armed forces and much of the free world during the 1940s. In the 1950s, Minute Maid and Snow Crop, both of which had started out separately to produce and market frozen juice, merged under the Minute Maid name and added a frozen vegetable line. The frozen vegetables were co-packed for Minute Maid by a California food processor. Jack Seabrook, C.F.'s youngest son, who was elected president of the company in 1954, saw an opportunity: "Minute Maid was losing money on vegetables, had swollen vegetable inventories and unhappy banks, including some of the same banks which were unhappy with our inventory. I had the audacious idea of offering to liquidate the large Minute Maid brand vegetable inventory for the banks in return for Minute Maid going out of the vegetable business." The banks liked the idea, and, in 1957, Seabrook Farms assumed the Minute Maid inventory and put that company out of business. By 1959, Seabrook Farms had higher sales volume and made much more money than ever before in the history of the company.[39]

Ironically and sadly, 1959 also was the year when Seabrook Farms, which had been nurtured and expanded since 1913, changed hands and began a gradual slide into oblivion. C.F., nearly eighty in the spring of 1959, apparently neither understood nor appreciated his son Jack's attempts at making the company a major player among an increasing number of competitors nationwide. In any event, C.F., the primary shareholder in the business he started, sold to Seeman Brothers what amounted to the guts of Seabrook Farms. The company went downhill gradually at first and then rapidly. Seeman Brothers later sold the company to Spring Mills, which was unable to halt the decline.[40]

On Wednesday, March 31, 1982, the *Bridgeton Evening News* marked an important occasion with its page-one headline, "So long, Seabrook." The article continued, "The last ninety-seven workers . . . will collect their final paycheck today."[41] The "biggest vegetable factory on earth" and the proud possessor of three significant firsts in the history of New Jersey and American agriculture was no more.

🕷 Major Food Processors Go West

While Seabrook Farms faded away, most of the other major food processors moved away—to California primarily, where the sun shines warmer and longer. By the time Spring Mills padlocked Seabrook Farms, Campbell Soup Company, H. J. Heinz, P. J. Ritter, Del Monte, and other major canneries had relocated their production facilities outside New Jersey. Although the year-round growing season in such states as California and Florida was a reason why food processors left New Jersey, it wasn't the only one—perhaps not even the most important one for some companies. Processors complained that the cost of doing business in New Jersey was excessive due largely to the fact that operating expenses for both them and the Garden State farmers who supplied them were inflated by being in such close proximity to the high-priced markets of New York and Philadelphia. They also cited New Jersey's air pollution laws, which were stricter than those in other states, as a reason for heading west.[42]

The passing of the P. J. Ritter Company is a case in point.

P. J. Ritter Company and other food processors started thinking of California and elsewhere as World War II came to an end. "[California] production methods were extremely efficient," wrote Paul J. Ritter III. "Farmers tilled their lands using land surveys in order to obtain the proper slopes to irrigate them. Also, the growing season was dry in California, which enabled the tomatoes to remain on the vine until they were all ripe. This allowed mechanical harvesting, which reduced labor costs. Moreover, because of the infrequent rains, irrigation systems were necessary, allowing the California grower the ability to apply precise amounts of moisture for optimum growth. In contrast, although . . . Rutgers University

developed a tough skinned tomato that could be harvested me-
chanically, often rains bogged down the equipment, making such
harvesting impossible."[43]

The Ritter plant in Bridgeton had been built on the bank of the
Cohansey River, which allowed barges to bring tomatoes from
Delaware and Maryland, but the river also was where tomato waste
from processing was dumped. New antipollution regulations in the
1960s ended that method of disposal, even after Ritter had introduced a screen to remove most of the solid particles from wastewater. In cooperation with Hunt Foods, another processor, Ritter
built a pipeline that carried the tomato effluent into a receiving
tank located on a farmer's field several miles away. There, after another screening, the wastewater was pumped into a sprinkler system that spread the effluent over farm fields. This disposal system
cost over one million dollars. Government clean air regulations
also placed a financial burden on the company. For example, the
plant's furnace was oil fired, and smokestack discharges were considered to be unacceptable pollutants; furthermore, the state Department of Environmental Protection required Ritter to remove
its large oil tanks that were located near the river's edge.[44]

In 1967, a banner year for the company despite new government regulations, Ritter turned 36,000 tons of Jersey tomatoes
into its "catsup" brand and processed 90 percent of the asparagus
sold in glass jars in America. But Jersey asparagus was in trouble.
A root disease, fulcirium wilt, was beginning to attack fields of asparagus throughout the state. Another problem was the increasing
cost of processing asparagus. When asparagus production was at
its peak, it took over 200,000 man-hours and 250 workers to process the vegetable.

Finally, in 1974, the state ordered Ritter to cover the entire
180-foot production line to protect the operation from any foreign
objects floating in the air. The company could not make up the
cost of installing such an addition because of the reduced production of asparagus, so, on Friday, April 4, 1975, Ritter shut down,
necessitating the scrapping of $250,000 worth of asparagus pro-
cessing equipment.[45]

In some ways, the most hurtful occurrence among many during the Ritter Company's waning days in New Jersey was when

people living downwind from the plant complained about the aroma of cooking tomatoes. "This was the smell of prosperity and employment," Paul Ritter III wrote, "and now it was considered a public nuisance."[46]

On the other hand and at about the same time, the residents of Salem were longing to get a whiff of the same odor that once emanated from the H. J. Heinz ketchup plant that had recently closed, putting hundreds out of work. The city government was especially distressed because Heinz had, two years before shutting down, talked the governing body into leveling rows of houses of another era so that Heinz could expand its plant. Some forty years after Heinz moved out of town and out of New Jersey, Ron LeHew, a longtime Salem resident, reminisced about that aroma in his semiweekly column in the county newspaper, *Today's Sunbeam*: "When one grew up in Salem, any activity during the autumn was accompanied by the warm, sweet spice of tomatoes being processed into Heinz ketchup at the Griffith Street plant. . . . It seemingly was everywhere and around you at all times. It was there as you glumly called an end to summer and grudgingly went off to school. It was there during afternoon recess on the playground. And it was there as you shuffled home through fallen leaves on golden, sun-beamed autumn afternoons."[47]

▓ Canning and Freezing Survive

The aroma may still be smelled in Williamstown. Violet Packing Company, the oldest continuously running tomato-canning operation in America and the last such plant in the Garden State, processed nearly 19,000 tons of tomatoes from 750 New Jersey acres in the 2004 season. Not only is Violet Packing Company alive and cooking (now under new ownership), but the Seabrook Farms name is still found in your favorite supermarket's frozen food section on boxes of creamed spinach. Seabrook Brothers & Sons, the successor to Seabrook Farms, now annually produces the same number of pounds of frozen foods—one hundred million—that Seabrook Farms turned out at its peak in the 1950s.

Seabrook Brothers & Sons had its beginning even before the last Seabrook Farms employee took home his or her last paycheck.

C.F.'s two grandsons, James and Charles, worked for Seabrook Farms when it was called Seabrook Foods and owned by Spring Mills. James was president of the northern division of Spring Mills in 1975 when Spring Mills executives talked of closing the old Seabrook Farms operation in Upper Deerfield. "I was opposed to the decision," said James in an interview, "and I made a nuisance of myself, coming up with plans and projections [for saving the plant]. I continued to pursue my case until I alienated [top management], which wasn't hard to do. Spring Mills didn't want to hear any more about [my plans], so I quit, or I got fired. It's pretty hard to tell which it was. That was in August 1977. I was unemployed and had no prospects, but I got to thinking if I really believed in all the projections I had made, why not go ahead and do it. My brother and I put up $100,000 and we ultimately borrowed about $20 million to build a new plant."[48] The new business froze its first batch of green beans on July 14, 1978.

Today, Seabrook Brothers & Sons operates out of a modern facility a few miles south of the old Seabrook Farms plant down the railroad spur built by C.F. According to James Seabrook, Jr., now president of Seabrook Brothers & Sons and one of the five sons in the business, the company has 283 customers, which include a number of the major supermarket chains and the huge Sysco food distributor; the most popular of the approximately thirty frozen vegetables packed and marketed by Seabrook Brothers & Sons are green beans and spinach. In fact, said Seabrook, when shoppers anywhere pick up any brand of frozen dinner, if it contains spinach, the chances are very good the spinach came from Seabrook Brothers & Sons.

Although one of the reasons other major food processors gave for deserting New Jersey for California was a longer growing season, Seabrook is quick to point out that the season in Salem and Cumberland counties is from April to November. "People don't think of New Jersey as being south, but if you go south of here you're below the latitude of Baltimore. So, our farmers can double or triple crop. We compete with the spinach growing areas of Texas, California, and Mexico."

Unlike Seabrook Farms, which owned and planted thousands of acres of farmland, Seabrook Brothers & Sons does not farm.

However, the company uses its own equipment and personnel to harvest crops on farms that raise vegetables under contract to the company. "It's all done by machines—our machines, so the farmers don't have to buy the equipment themselves. In some cases, we even let farmers use our planting machines," said James Seabrook, Jr.

Harrison Woodhull Crosby and the mom-and-pop businesses that, more than a century ago, found a way to put tomatoes and other vegetables in bottles and cans would be pleased today. A food processing industry that has seen better days is looking ahead to better days.

"A Decent Home for Every American Family" 🌸 CHAPTER 3

The date was June 22, 1944, a Thursday, slightly more than two weeks after the Allied invasion on the coast of Normandy and a little less than fifteen months from the end of World War II. President Franklin Delano Roosevelt sat at a desk surrounded by members of Congress and the American Legion and, with a sweeping and heavy stroke of ten pens, signed into law the Servicemen's Readjustment Act—the GI Bill of Rights. In so doing, he changed forever where and how American families would live.

Many of those families would leave small, rented apartments in the cities at war's end and move into small, cookie-cutter houses they owned on land where once grew tomatoes or potatoes, where cows once chewed grass, where row upon row of trees once stood, their branches brought low by apples or peaches. In the fifties and sixties, tens of thousands of farm acres in America disappeared under cement blocks and black macadam.

The statistics are incredible and historic. In the United States, the number of families who owned homes increased from 44 percent in 1940 to 60 percent by 1960, the greatest increase over a comparable period of time before or since in the 230 years we have existed as a nation. For example, from 1960 to 2000, a forty-year period, the number went up only 6 percentage points. The numbers for New Jersey are even more astounding. In 1940, only 39 percent of families owned homes; twenty years later, the number had ballooned to 61 percent.

Where were all those New Jersey houses built? During that same period, from 1940 to 1960, the Garden State lost 470,000 farm acres. By 1970, only ten years later, an additional 409,000 farm acres had disappeared, for a whopping total of 879,000—close to a million farm acres gone in just three decades!

The laws that brought about this cataclysmic change in American life and to the American landscape in the decades following the end of World War II were initially drafted out of fear as much as out of gratitude for the sacrifices of our men and women in uniform. Early in 1944, when it first became possible to hope that the Allies would ultimately vanquish the armed forces of Imperial Japan and Nazi Germany, the federal government considered what might happen in and to the nation when, sooner rather than later, fifteen million and more servicemen and women would become veterans looking for new jobs and new places to live. Many of the lawmakers in 1944 were also in the capital that day in 1932 when thousands of out-of-work World War I veterans marched on Washington in a desperate effort to lay immediate claim to promised government war bonuses that as yet had not been paid. No one wanted a repeat of that event, especially since the number of veterans from World War II would be considerably greater than the number of World War I veterans.

Therefore, in an effort to cushion the impact of returning veterans on a society and economy trying to recover from four years of war, and in an attempt to head off any threat of civil unrest posed by jobless and homeless veterans, politicians and big business put their brains together and drafted this historic law.[1]

The GI Bill of Rights, which some historians have termed the last and perhaps greatest deal of FDR's New Deal, relieved the pressure on postwar America primarily in two ways. First, by offering a free college education to every veteran who wanted one, the GI Bill effectively siphoned off on to college campuses and into training schools men who otherwise might have dangerously overloaded the job market in an economy trying to readjust to peacetime. By 1955, ten years after war's end, more than two million veterans had attended college and another seven million had received school or job training. Second, by offering generous loans toward the purchase of new homes, the GI Bill helped to ensure stable families where a significant portion of income that otherwise might be needed to pay down a mortgage instead could be used to pay the costs of raising children and toward the purchase both of life's necessities and some of its luxuries.

Only in a very few instances in the long history of the nation has a law so drastically and indelibly shaped the kind of society in which Americans live and work. The GI Bill helped veterans, many of whom had been renters prior to the war, to purchase a small, two-bedroom house that was so typical of almost all of the postwar developments. Furthermore, the GI Bill's provisions offering a free college education and/or job training prepared veterans to take their place in a postwar economy and lifestyle that was, in many ways, very different from what they had left when they shipped off to Europe or Asia.[2]

✳ *New Suburbs Grow in Farmers' Fields*

The suburban sprawl of the 1950 and '60s that replaced plows with Caterpillars in the hinterland was chiefly propelled, of course, by a combination of the GI Bill and the later Housing Act of 1949. The Housing Act, which had as its goal "a decent home and suitable living environment for every American family," placed billions more dollars into the hands of home-buying, family-building veterans via the Federal Housing Authority and Fannie Mae.

However, suburban sprawl also was fueled by Americans' pride and joy—not a baby in diapers but a car with fluid drive and ostentatious fins. Whereas old, established suburbs close in to the city flourished because of their proximity to railroad tracks, the new suburbs that sprouted in fields and orchards far from the iron rails depended upon new highways that would carry men and women in new cars either into the city or, just as likely, to a business or industry that recently had vacated the city to be closer to the newborn communities where many of the employees now lived.

The manufacture of civilian cars had ceased in 1942 when Ford, General Motors, and other automakers put jeeps, halftracks, and tanks on their assembly lines. By early 1946, however, it was back to normal for the manufacturers, but normal now meant astronomical numbers of cars never before realized let alone imagined and—introduced in the 1950s—air-conditioning, power this and power that, and levers a driver could push to indicate a turn. No more sticking one's arm out the window in a monsoon or blizzard. New car sales in 1949, three years after the resumption of civilian manufacture, totaled nearly 5 million. By the mid-fifties, sales approached 7.2 million.

Not only were car manufacturers annually turning out millions of cars and station wagons (11 percent of production in 1956), but federal and state governments acting in concert (with 90 percent federal dollars) were laying down more and more asphalt to carry the cars from the new suburbs to wherever their drivers and passengers wanted to go—and more directly and quickly than ever before. A series of Federal-Aid Highway Acts, beginning in 1944 and culminating in 1956, authorized the construction of a new interstate highway system that, eventually, would add more than 46,000 miles of roads that were at least two lanes in both directions and able to accommodate vehicles driving at speeds as high as seventy miles per hour.

Knowing, as we do now, how millions of veterans and their families in postwar America moved lock, stock, and often half-filled barrels into developments that forever covered over land that first had been tilled by Native Americans, it seems especially nescient on the part of the U.S. Department of Agriculture to conclude Part 2 of its 1940 Yearbook as follows:

> Higher consumption per capita and more nonfarm employment are cures for the ailments both of the agricultural land and of the agricultural people. They are the cures for urban ailments, too. [The urban dweller] has a vital interest in the distribution of the people on the land, in the relationship they have to it, in the use they make of it, and in the amount and distribution of the resulting

farm income. This interest involves him inevitably in important land use responsibilities.[3]

As we will note in other chapters of this book, it wasn't until much later, long after the postwar rush on farmland and two decades of suburban sprawl that urban dwellers or anyone with political foresight and power seriously considered how to properly exercise "important land use responsibilities." Indeed, during the period from 1946 through at least the sixties, suburban sprawl pretty much erased the historic patterns of land use. Housing developments were neither designed nor implemented in response to the organic integrity and physical characteristics of the land. Developers merely bulldozed into submission land that generations of farmers had tilled until that day when the generation of the middle years of the twentieth century succumbed to the very real pressure to sell the land and provide homes for deserving and ambitious veterans and their young families.

✿ New Housing Invades Bergen County

At the very beginning of suburban sprawl in New Jersey, developers set their sights and plot maps on Bergen County across the Hudson River from Manhattan, where hardy Dutch settlers had groomed their fruitful plantations three centuries earlier. Just before the invasion by armies of bulldozers and flat-bed trucks laden with two-by-fours, Bergen County was still noted for its produce. More than six hundred families owned farms in 1948 and produced bumper crops. The New Jersey Department of Agriculture estimated that Bergen's 5,540 cultivated acres produced 34,584 tons of vegetables. Most of Bergen's vegetables were marketed in New York City, a practice reminiscent, of course, to the time two centuries earlier when Dutch families working the same ground sold their produce across the Hudson River. The major differences by the middle of the twentieth century were that there was much more produce to sell and farmers took what they had to market in trucks instead of wagons.[4]

However, developers and realtors hoping to build and sell as many houses as possible to as many new families as possible increasingly pressured Bergen's farmers to give up the land they had inherited from their own ancestors and from the Leni-Lenape families that had first scratched a living from it. By 1970, therefore, housing, offices, shopping malls, industries, and major highways had pretty nearly covered over the once fertile fields, and farming was relegated to history books and became the subject of tall tales told to children by their grandparents.[5]

The borough of Paramus occupies the center of Bergen County, and, in the late 1940s and early '50s, it was especially appealing to developers. Its fruitful farms were bordered by two state highways, Routes 4 and 17, that could provide new home dwellers with easy access to New York City. Not at all incidentally, they also led to new businesses and industries attracted to the area by a burgeoning population that included a number of recent college graduates (courtesy of the GI Bill) who were charting a future where they would eventually assume leadership in those businesses and industries—and in government at all levels.

The official Paramus Web site includes a historical piece titled "Paramus Memories." It invited the reader to "close your eyes and imagine for a moment a farm community nestled in the heart of Bergen County. Picture a peaceful community comprised of black dirt (muck) and upland farms with acres of celery, corn, tomatoes, spinach, eggplant, pepper and a variety of vegetables as far as the eye can see. There are greenhouses and barns, trucks and tractors dotting the landscape along with chicken and dairy farms. This is Paramus eighty years ago."

True, but one doesn't have to go back that far to envision the farms of Paramus. I saw them as a child growing up in neighboring Ridgewood, and in the summer of 1947, at the conclusion of junior high, I pulled radishes on Richard Scoskie's farm on Paramus Road (land now occupied by Bergen Community College). I got up very early in the morning, earnestly prayed for rain, then, disappointed that my prayer was not answered, got on my bike and pedaled several miles to the Scoskie farm. I confess that I was not very accomplished as a farmhand, but, as I look back, it was an unappreciated privilege to dirty my hands in soil that may have been scratched hard by a Leni-Lenape woman and later planted in an orderly fashion by a Dutchman who might have been a Tory or a Whig.

Two years after my forgettable summer as a farm laborer, Henry Behnke sold his farm east of Sprout Creek to a developer, who promptly halted the sixty-third harvest of corn, tomatoes, and cabbage from land settled in the late nineteenth century by Behnke's father, a German immigrant. The developer then planted 135 all-of-a-kind houses, each with its own septic tank. It was the first postwar development in Paramus and one of the first in Bergen County and New Jersey. By the end of the sixties, the borough that had boasted 100 percent farmland for nearly three hundred years had lost 100 percent of its farmland.

In the fall of 2004, Henry Behnke's nephew, Fritz, then age eighty-six, presided over what remains of Paramus's agricultural legacy, mostly equipment farmers used in their fields and assorted appliances and devices employed by their wives in the homestead, all of it contained in the aptly named Paramus Fritz Behnke Historical Museum. The borough converted a groundskeeper's house on Paramus Golf Course into the museum, whose artifacts are neatly displayed on two crowded levels. Much of what there is to see, including the Eggomatic invented by another of his uncles that could weigh and sort eighteen hundred eggs an hour, was collected by Behnke over a period of fifteen years and first housed in the barn behind his house on Farview Avenue.

Before everything was moved into the museum, Behnke frequently opened the century-old barn doors to children and showed them the legacy he had preserved. Then they would go outside to stand in the yard, and Behnke would sweep his arms in a wide arc and exclaim, "Look around as far as you can see; all of this land was our family's farm." Of course, house upon house upon house was all the children could now see.

The official museum hours are between one and five on Sunday afternoons, but Behnke was on duty many weekdays guiding twenty-first-century schoolchildren past never-before-seen contraptions such as a push hoe ("I walked behind one for years; every time the plow hit a rock, I'd get the wind knocked out of me"). The tour for children usually ended with a ten-minute film, but before they entered the little theater, they had to walk close by a small display that reminded them that the cereal they ate for breakfast originated in a corn or wheat field, and the syrup their mothers used in cooking probably began as soy beans in a farmer's field.

The Behnke brothers—Fritz's father and his two uncles—farmed a combined total of 150 acres during World War II. Fritz was deferred because farming was considered an essential wartime industry. He remembered running a tractor in those years from dawn to ten or eleven o'clock at night, headlamps lighting the way. "Paramus, then, was basically two different types of farming," he recalled. "On the east side of Sprout Brook, which pretty much runs north and south through the center of town, was upland farming—sandy loam—where we raised our corn, tomatoes, and cabbage. Everything went to the market at night. On the west side was the low land, mostly used for raising celery. Paramus was known as the celery capital in those days, you know."

Then the war was over, and the boys were coming home, and home for thousands of veterans and their new families was in Paramus. After his uncle sold his share of the 150 acres jointly owned by the brothers, Behnke's father was next. "My pop tried to hold out. He did not want to sell; he wanted to farm. He loved farming. But one farm after another was being sold. Pop's health was not too good, and he asked me if I wanted to keep the farm. I said I'd ask my wife, and she said no. So, I said to Pop, 'Sell it.' He got $750 an acre." Behnke remembers when the houses sprouted in the cabbage patch and the cornfield and where the tomatoes once grew on vines. "Each had a kitchen, living room and two bedrooms. And, of course, a bathroom. The houses sold from $7,000 to $10,000 in the beginning."

In 1952, the *Newark Sunday News* reported what happened in and to Paramus after the Behnke brothers and some of their neighbors sold their farmland in the late forties:

> The boom reached its peak in 1950 when 1,030 homes valued at about $10,000,000 were constructed. The boom leveled off in 1951, but picked up again this year. There are now six developments under construction, with the largest, Midland Knolls at Route 17 and Midland Avenue, scheduled to have more than 200 homes when completed. A spurt is expected soon from the projected plans of L. Bamberger & Co. of Newark and Allied Stores,

Inc. of New York. Bam's has disclosed its intention of building a mammoth shopping center in Paramus at the juncture of Routes 4 and 17. Allied Stores is planning a similar venture [on] Route 4 between Spring Valley Road and Farview Avenue.[6]

The "spurt" culminated in the Garden State Plaza, which, at two million square feet was, in 2005, still the largest mall in New Jersey and the Bergen Mall on Route 4. Three other malls have been added since, for a total of five, more than in any other town of the same size in New Jersey.

When I covered Paramus as a reporter for *The Record* of Bergen County in the late fifties, I often consulted with Fred Bogert on matters pertaining to the history of the borough. He was, for example, the primary authority in the region on Dutch settlements and Dutch genealogy. In 1961, he finally put most of what he knew into a book about the borough, and he pretty much condensed into a paragraph the spectacular and often traumatic transformation from tranquil farming center into Bergen's frantic heartbeat:

> The vast acreage which had been devoted to farming, or was lying fallow, would begin to serve a different purpose. Booming and blossoming throughout every section, every corner of town, would come houses in great profusion. And with these houses, new schools, new streets, a library, tremendous shopping centers and, most important of all, a population increase beyond the conception of the earliest settlers.[7]

Bogert didn't exaggerate. In just ten years, from 1950 to 1960, the population increased by 271 percent, from 6,268 to 23,238. The *Newark Sunday News* article in 1952 called attention to the impact that acres of new, young, and growing families was having on the community. It reported that 350 children entered the school system in September of that year, bringing total enrollment to 1,600. Three years earlier, enrollment had been half that number. In less than two years, the school board, which not too long before had been responsible for only two small schools, was forced to build an additional twenty-six classrooms at a cost of about $1 million.[8] In 1953, the year after the *Newark Sunday News* article, 100 students graduated from eighth grade (Paramus did not yet have its own high school) and 400 children entered kindergarten.

In addition to facing an immediate crisis in classroom space, the borough also was confronted with the need to build a townwide sewerage system to replace the septic tanks. In 1951, the House of Representatives authorized an investigation into whether government loan guarantees were being used to pay for inferior housing that was mushrooming all over the country. William B. Widnall, Republican legislator from Bergen County and a member of the House Banking and Currency Committee, headed the probe. One of the subcommittee's first stops was Paramus, where nearly three hundred complaints had been received from homeowners, many of whom reported that the septic tanks installed by builders were inadequate. Although the Widnall subcommittee did find that many complaints were valid, Fritz Behnke, looking back from 2004, believed the problem had more to do with the families moving into the borough from New York City, Jersey City, and other urban areas. "If they came from the city, they were used to running the water and flushing when they pleased, but when they came here they didn't realize that a septic tank only absorbs so much water. So, the tanks would back up."

When Behnke was asked whether Paramus and Bergen County should have been more prescient at the end of World War II and saved some of the farmland, he replied, "You can't stop progress; you can only delay it. When these people—whether they were [veterans] or just people coming out of the city—needed more land, it just got swallowed up—the whole area. The reason Paramus was swallowed up so fast was because there was so much land in Paramus, and it was cheap to buy. We never thought we were going to run out of land."

A planning essay written for the Bergen County Department of Planning and Economic Development in 1989 looked back to the beginnings of suburban sprawl and echoed Fritz Behnke:

> Because land was cheap in rural areas, builders "leapfrogged" past growing suburbs in order to make suburban life accessible to more and more Americans. Planners joke that subdivisions are named for the biozones they displace. So, moving up came, for

many others, to mean finding an affordable house in a more remote suburb. The contact with nature, along with the cheaper space, the low taxes and the good schools, justified the longer commute. "Out there," we figured, there would always be new land to bring gently into the overall equation. Planners always looked to this unused land—we still refer to open spaces as "undeveloped" land—as the resource that would redress the social and economic distortions that the existing stock of land had failed to address. [However], while bountiful resources drove the suburb-building process, more limited resources now dominate our thought processes. Who would have thought, thirty years ago, that quiet suburbs would today be suffering from such mounting congestion?[9]

🎋 Levitt Transforms Willingboro

Paramus was already booming when, in 1954, William J. Levitt set off an even greater housing and subsequent population explosion in rural Burlington County. A lieutenant in the Seabees during World War II, Levitt had impressed admirals and generals with his uncanny ability to turn a patch of Pacific island disfigured by bomb craters and flamethrowers into a usable airfield practically overnight. By the middle of the 1950s, his name was synonymous with even greater achievements: thousands of mass-produced houses in developments that bore his name in Hempstead, Long Island, and Bucks County, Pennsylvania. By the time Levitt descended on Willingboro Township, his modus operandi was well established: "Just beg, borrow, or steal the money and then build and build."[10]

Two hundred and seventy-seven years before Levitt's agents came knocking on the doors of farmhouses, the 4,900 acres they eventually purchased were known as Wellingborough, so named in 1677 by William Penn's Quaker agents. The Quakers "purchased" the land from the local Leni-Lanape chiefs for the prix fixe of six matched coats, guns, hatchets, and kettles. They established spacious and prosperous plantations inland from the Delaware River, about sixteen miles upriver from Philadelphia, and along the

Rancocas Creek, a navigable tributary that emptied into the Delaware and formed the southern boundary of the township. During the eighteenth and nineteenth centuries, the plantations were subdivided into a few very large parcels and a number of smaller farms. The land was very fertile and produced great harvests of New Jersey sweet corn and a number of other vegetables and fruits. Rancocas Creek and other, smaller streams allowed farmers to ship their produce on barges down the Delaware River to Philadelphia and Camden markets.[11]

To claim that Wellingborough remained an almost static rural enclave for two and one half centuries would be an understatement. Considering how the New York and Philadelphia metropolitan areas expanded, particularly in the decades after the Civil War, it seems almost incomprehensible that the population of Wellingborough increased by less than 100 persons in 120 years, from 782 in 1830 to 852 in 1950. As amazing as that statistic is, however, even more mind-boggling are the population numbers for the next twenty years. By 1970, when the Levitt housing blitz was winding down, the population of Willingboro (the name had been changed twice, first to Levittown) had soared to 43,414!

What made those 4,900 bucolic acres so ripe for the plucking by Levitt? Herbert Gans, who lived in Wellingborough-Levittown-Willingboro during the first two years of the historic transformation, offered this explanation:

Not long after the Bucks County development had gotten off to a successful start, the [Levitt] firm began to consider yet a third Levittown, and this time it sought to eliminate the difficulties it had encountered previously by purchasing land within a single township. Ultimately, the choice fell on Willingboro Township. . . . Willingboro Township was an area of small farms, producing peaches, plums, and tomatoes on the region's sandy soil. It was particularly suitable for Levitt and Sons because it was inhabited only by individual farmers, a few owners of what had once been a summer home colony, and the village of Rancocas, a nineteenth-century Quaker settlement of less than five hundred people. Soon after the firm bought the land, it had the township boundaries changed so that Rancocas was incorporated into the neighboring township of Westhampton. Once Rancocas had been moved out, only about six hundred people were left in the township, and they, the builder felt, could be persuaded to give him a free hand to build as he wished. Willingboro would provide a virtual tabula rasa [unparalleled opportunity] for realizing William Levitt's goals and plans.[12]

✳ *Farming Becomes a Business*

The post–World War II years brought prosperity to the country in general, but many farmers did not or could not share in the good times. By 1950, farming in Willingboro and almost everywhere else in America had changed from being a way of life for a farming family to being a business—agribusiness. The individual farmer who, for decades, had survived by growing a variety of vegetables and fruits on his two or three dozen acres and either selling them locally, at auction, or under contract to a processor now discovered that, in order to pay his bills and make a little profit (always a challenge for farmers), he had to specialize in whatever agricultural products were in greatest demand by consumers (and change with the demands). This specialization—sometimes referred to as niche farming—is more fully discussed in Chapter Seven.

Whether the farmer turned to specialization or not, postwar agribusiness required a greater capital investment in machinery and buildings in which to store that equipment. One reason why farmers turned to expensive mechanical means for planting, cultivating, and harvesting crops was because, in the decades after the war, it became even more costly to hire, house, and feed the number of farm laborers required to perform the same functions. It has been estimated that farmers in America may have as much as a trillion dollars invested in buildings, equipment, and other assets.

Writing in the early 1970s, a decade and more after owners of small farms in Willingboro and elsewhere had already faced the challenges of modern agribusiness, Hubert Schmidt stated, "Farmers near the breaking point as to operating profits simply cannot afford the additions to their labor bill brought by wage increases. Their alternative to quitting [and selling out to developers], if they can raise the capital, is to mechanize still further, hoping that the costly machinery will pay for itself by eliminating field hands."[13] Meeting the new demands of agribusiness required farmers to become more skilled in finance, especially in the management of larger bank loans required for the mechanization. In order to compete in more specialized markets, farmers often needed to learn new production techniques and marketing practices. The expansion and modernization of agriculture revitalized old companies that served farmers and spawned new ones. These companies began manufacturing a host of new chemicals designed to better fertilize crops and protect them from damaging insects and disease. The farmer had to keep up with these developments and, of course, find a way to pay for new products.

As agribusiness boomed across America, state and federal government regulations also grew—and grew. For the first time, the farmer-businessman had to learn and comply with directives on how to use the new insecticides and pesticides on the market, how to conserve water used for irrigation, how to manage employees, and so on. The paperwork mounted and farmers found it necessary to learn how to use computers in order to keep up and to avoid making mistakes that could result in reducing whatever slim profit they were able to realize in the new marketplace.

The new demands of agribusiness were more than some farmers were willing to accept. When Levitt's agents, therefore, drove up Willingboro's country lanes in the mid-fifties with their offer to buy good, productive farmland, many individual farmers owning small farms were ready to give up a way of life that had turned into an expensive business they couldn't afford to operate any longer. It cannot be said that the Levitts bore full responsibility for putting farmers out of business. Already at work in Willingboro and elsewhere were new and often costly farming methods and market demands that made it difficult for the small family farm to remain productive and solvent.[14]

The buying and selling began in 1954 when a firm of Philadelphia lawyers contacted country lawyer Alexander Denbo at his office in Burlington City and asked him to help an unidentified client purchase three hundred or so Willingboro acres for an undisclosed purpose. "The first farmers he attacked were those who owed money," said Isaac Van Sciver III, a retired farmer who, at age eighty-one, sat with his wife in the sunroom of their home in Edgewater Park across Route 130 from Willingboro on a sunless afternoon in December 2004 and rewound memories back fifty years. Denbo, at the time, was solicitor for Willingboro Township and surely would have had knowledge of farmer families in debt.

Van Sciver is descended from a long line of Van Scivers who settled in the area three hundred years ago. In the 1600s, three brothers, who spelled their name the Dutch way—Van Schiver—drifted down from southern New York State and joined the Quaker farmers who had purchased Wellingborough from the Leni-Lenape. In 1950, the line still included three brothers: Oscar, Charles and Isaac, Jr., who, not so coincidentally, married three Snyder sisters. The brothers each farmed twenty to thirty acres close to Route 130, which was then known as Route 25 and before that as the Burlington-Camden Pike. Oscar's and Charles's spreads were in Willingboro, and Isaac's farm was across the highway (then two lanes) in Edgewater Park. When the first Van Scivers made their home in the area, Edgewater Park was part of Wellingborough. The brothers grew a variety of vegetables, and, in the years immediately after World War II, they still plowed, planted, and harvested walking behind a single horse or team. Like the postwar farmers Hubert Schmidt described, they had neither specialized in their farm produce nor mechanized their operation. They were, then, prime targets for Denbo et al., who came calling with papers to sign and checks ready to be cashed.

Not all farmers accepted Levitt's first offer, Van Sciver said. Some held out, not necessarily for more money, but because they wanted to continue to farm. What finally convinced many of the holdouts to sell their property, he said, were the complaining new homeowners transplanted from urban areas, coupled with Levitt's decision to up the price he was willing to pay for their farmland. Many of the families from urban areas who moved into Levitt's houses entertained a romantic notion about living in the country and away from the city, but, as it turned out, most didn't like the sounds and smells of the country. A family would move into a house next door to a farmer's irrigation hole, Van Sciver said, not realizing that the water pump might whoosh and whir until midnight or beyond. Other new arrivals got bent out of shape—actually frightened—when a biplane swooped down out of the sky and nearly brushed the tassels of the corn it was dusting.

Again echoing Hubert Schmidt, Van Sciver said that, in the early fifties, most of the summer farm labor came out of Philadelphia and was housed in what Van Sciver called "rough," cheaply built quarters. By the end of the decade, however, and into the sixties, when most of the farm labor came from Puerto Rico and Jamaica, the New Jersey Department of Labor insisted on better living conditions for migrant labor. New construction, of course, led to the farmer's age-old problem: insufficient capital and a reduction in profits.

In 1960, after his father died and his mother sold the family farm (the old irrigation hole is now the drainage area for an age-55-plus housing development), Van Sciver purchased twenty-five acres and rented another thirty-five acres in Edgewater Park across Route 130 from Willingboro. Instead of raising a variety of vegetables for the open market as most of the Willingboro farmers before him had been doing when Levitt came along and gobbled up their land, he decided to specialize: sweet corn for roadside stands (he didn't have a stand himself). Also, Van Sciver was one of the first farmers in the region to purchase an automatic corn picker. He specialized and mechanized and made a decent profit.

Van Sciver began cutting corn as early as June 29 in a good year, and that meant his farm could supply sweet corn for the plethora of backyard picnics scheduled on and about the fourth of July. In its best years, the Van Sciver farm supplied sweet corn to thirty-two roadside stands in New Jersey, northeastern Pennsylvania, southeastern New York State and as far north as Darien, Connecticut. "The corn in those other states normally wasn't ready to cut until after July 4," Van Sciver said. The roadside stands wanted to tell their customers that the corn they offered was picked that very morning (talk about Jersey Fresh!), so the Van Sciver cutting machine turned on at midnight and went through the night. "The trucks from the roadside stands started arriving at twelve o'clock and lined up along our long lane and spilled out into the road," said Ruth Jean Van Sciver.

Van Sciver finally gave up farming in the winter of 1982 after crushing the bones in one leg in an accident. "My doctor told me not to farm the following spring and summer, and it felt so good not farming for a year I didn't go back." Perhaps the real reason he didn't resume farming the next year was because he and his wife believed that if he couldn't supply the roadside stands for an entire summer, they would have to go elsewhere to get their sweet corn and, if they did, they might not ever come back to the Van Sciver farm. As the calendar turned over into 2005, the Van Scivers were still surrounded by their twenty-five acres, which are no longer farmed, and were content. "It's been a good life," said Van Sciver, "a very good life."

In the second week of October 1958, two years before the Van Scivers purchased their twenty-five acres in Edgewater Park, the first families moved into their new Levitt-built homes on land in Willingboro where once a farmer might have grown tomatoes for the Campbell Soup Company or cabbage that a plant in Philadelphia turned into sauerkraut. It had taken Levitt and his agents nearly four years to buy all the land. The New Jersey Levittown differed from those on Long Island and in Bucks County in several ways, the most important difference being that, in Willingboro, the firm offered three styles of houses instead of only one: the traditional four-bedroom Cape Cod selling for $11,500; a three-bedroom, one-story rancher for $13,000; and a two-story colonial with three or four bedrooms costing either $14,000 or $14,500.

Levitt invented the mass-produced house constructed in twenty-six steps. "Trucks stopped at each site [sixty-five-foot lots in Willingboro] to drop off identical, neatly bundled supplies: lumber, pipes, nails, shingles. Earthmovers appeared, dug for plumbing, and were followed by crews that performed a single phase of the construction. When they were finished, they moved on to the next house. Instead of the product moving down an assembly line, the assembly line moved along to the next product."[15] Levitt built his homes in sections, and in each section he built an elementary school. He also built a junior-senior high school to serve the new community. The streets in a section all began with the same letter. In one section, for example, families bought houses on courts named Grayson, Gaylord, Gunner, and Gallant. In another, the lanes were called Mariner, Medley, Melrose, and Melbourne.

Leonard Kimble was one farmer who resisted to the very end selling his land for houses, and he was one of the principal landowners in Willingboro. Isaac Van Sciver described him as an astute businessman who, "if there was a nickel to be made, he would make it." Kimble finally sold a small parcel of land to Levitt, but no houses were built upon it; today, the land is Willingboro's Fairmount Park. The Kimble family's large farm on Beverly-Rancocas Road, when it was finally sold, also became a park, one of the largest municipal parks in the state.[16]

🌸 The Housing Tsunami Rolls South

Imagine, if you will, a tidal wave bearing new houses and strip malls rising up in New Jersey at the end of World War II and crashing first onto Paramus's celery farms, then roaring west to inundate Willingboro's cornfields, and, more than a dozen years later, swelling once again to drown tomato farms and peach orchards in Washington Township, Gloucester County. In 1956, when farming was already a memory in Paramus and William Levitt was laying out houses by the hundreds, Hubert Read, Washington Township's police chief, had a two-way radio installed in his patrol car but complained that he didn't have anyone to talk to. When Chief Read was talking to himself, fewer than four thousand persons in this municipality of approximately twenty-three square miles depended on his protection. Many of them lived on one of nearly two hundred family farms spread among communities, or crossroads, called Bunker Hill, Chapel Heights, Cross Keys, Grenloch, Hurffville, Mayfair, and Turnersville. This was about the same number of farms that had existed in those locales in the late nineteenth century.

No one can say for sure why the tidal wave took so long to roll into Washington Township, but Anthony Demitrio of Weichert Realtors, one of the major real estate firms in the township, has a theory. The Walt Whitman Bridge and the Route 42 expressway opened in 1957 and offered the first direct connection between Philadelphia and the South Jersey municipalities south of Camden.

The older Benjamin Franklin Bridge served primarily as a link to communities east and north of Camden—Willingboro, for example. "However, for some unexplained reason," Demitrio said, "for a long time it was like someone had erected a stop sign on Route 42 at Bellmawr and Runnemede." It wasn't until the mid-sixties that families leaving Philadelphia and Camden and some of the older suburbs close in to those cities ventured beyond the "stop sign" and discovered Grenloch and Turnersville, the township communities located where the Route 42 expressway connects with Route 168, the old Blackhorse Pike.

Another, unidentified realtor was quoted in a 1986 news report as saying that he sold his first property in Washington Township—a split-level in Turnersville—in November 1963. The selling price was $14,500. He also recalled that the township had only one traffic light at the time. By 1967, the township's population had more than doubled, to approximately 12,000, but as late as 1976 real estate gurus weren't betting that the housing spurt of the late sixties would become a boom. Demitrio said he had a hard time in that year convincing Fred Fox, one of South Jersey's premier realtors (now deceased) to open an office in the township. "He didn't think there would be enough business."

It wasn't long before Fox and every other realtor in the area had more business than they could handle. By 1980, the population had more than doubled again, to 27,878. But the tidal wave hadn't begun to crest. When Route 55 opened to traffic in the mid-eighties, the remaining farmland of Washington Township and other municipalities in southern Gloucester County was fully exposed for the first time to a new crop of potential house buyers, and what they saw they liked.

As Washington Township began the year 2005, the tidal wave was almost spent and the population topped 48,000. And only two of two hundred farms remained. Joan Michael, the township's official historian, lamented the loss of farmland. "I taught for many years in this township, in second and third grades, and one thing I always would [ask] the children was, if we keep selling all our farms, where will our food come from? They, of course, replied that the food comes from the supermarket, but then I brought in cream in a tub and we churned the milk into butter in class. See, I would say, butter doesn't come from the supermarket; it comes from cream that comes from a cow that lives on a farm—here, in Washington Township."

Michael and her husband sell flowers and shrubs out of the greenhouse behind their modest home on two and three-quarter acres on Pitman-Downer Road. Across the heavily traveled road, on land where once peach trees flowered in the spring and bore fruit in the summer, Peachtree Condos have blossomed. The orchard next door to the Michaels' property has been converted into Plum Tree Estates. The Michaels used to grow and sell poinsettias at Christmas, but no longer. Poinsettias need to spend time in the dark, and when some residents of Plum Tree Estates installed floodlights in their backyards, that ended the poinsettia business. "We're trying to protect what we have left," said Michael, "but it's almost a losing cause. We've discovered that the people who live here now, for the most part, are too busy with their huge, expensive homes to have time for anything else, and they're really not into the township's history. This was a farming community that's now a bedroom community."

It is Joan Michael's task to acquaint the busy people with the township's history: twenty-one Leni-Lenape settlements; Underground Railroad escape tunnels on the old Turner property; and the Bell family, which grew—sort of—General Mills of Minneapolis from a 139-year-old grist mill in Washington Township.

Keeping the farming legacy alive in Washington Township is the chief responsibility of the Duffield family: father and mother, two sons, one daughter, two daughters-in-law, and a handful of grandchildren. By all accounts, the family is not only keeping the legacy alive, it is making sure that farming—sowing, reaping, marketing—is daily in the face of the busy people coming and going from their large, expensive homes. Duffield's Farm is one of the best illustrations of how, literally in the midst of sprawling housing developments, today's garden in the Garden State not only can withstand the pressure from developers who come calling with seven-digit checks in their deep pockets but can even turn a decent profit.

🐜 Keeping the Family Farm in the Family

It starts with family. You may recall Fritz Behnke in Paramus being asked by his aging father, who was under pressure to sell to a developer, whether he wanted to take over and continue to run the family farm, and his answer was no thanks. This exchange between parent and son or daughter is still played out in some fashion over coffee at the kitchen table or in the farm office throughout New Jersey—indeed, across the country. Increasingly, children of farmers go off to college and, after graduation, take jobs outside agriculture—almost certainly away from mother's and dad's or grandfather's farm. The problem, of course, is that mother and dad or grandfather are getting up in years and find it more and more difficult to manage what has become an agricultural business that is subject to more inconstant economic factors. The farmer who wants to retire from long hours and hard labor but has no heirs, or at least none interested in carrying on the business, becomes a particularly ripe prospect for developers and the realtors who represent them.

David Duffield, in his early seventies in 2005, knows that when he is ready to rest after more than fifty years of farming, his sons, David Jr. and Dan, will carry on. They already have primary responsibility for growing and harvesting thirty-five vegetables and fruits on 170 acres owned by the family and another 90 rented acres. Tracy, Dan's wife, kept a diary describing life on the Duffield Farm over twelve days in the fall of 2004 that was published in the December/January 2005 issue of *Farm & Ranch Living*. She recorded a few of the many responsibilities now shouldered by David Jr. and her husband. Here is an excerpt from the entry for September 11:

> The weather was beautiful. The guys pulled corn for the market, but were afraid we're short. The field they're picking is low and had standing water after a big rain. The guys also cut basil, pulled beets and radishes, and picked some peppers and squash. The last of the peaches were picked today, too. We direct-market our peaches—that's better than wholesale because we can name our own price.[17]

Earlier in this chapter, we also talked about how farmers in the postwar years who owned three or four dozen acres and were unable to or chose not to mechanize and specialize were most likely to succumb to the siren song of developers. Again, the Duffield Farm offers an example of how farmers can become more resilient to the temptations and pressures of suburban sprawl.

Although the elder Duffield has been farming since 1953—the year his father died and he graduated from high school—today's operation is very twenty-first century. While the farm does not specialize in what it grows, it has a singular marketing focus: the Duffield Farm Market at the busy intersection of Greentree and Chapel Heights Roads. "All that we grow is sold through the Farm Market," said Duffield. "We do not wholesale; we haven't, to speak of, since the late seventies." The Farm Market is no roadside stand. It approaches the size of some strip mall food stores and carries many of the same items. In addition to selling all the same-day-fresh vegetables and fruits grown on Duffields' 170 acres, the store has a deli that serves soup made by Duffield daughter Debbie and a bakery run by Ruth Ann, the wife of David, Jr.

Tracy is in charge of community outreach programs sponsored by the Farm Market that provide genuine services to families and, not incidentally, are, in Tracy's words, "great marketing tools," the kind of innovation in farming described in more detail in Chapter Seven. The Duffields' Learning Barn offers educational programs that annually involve upwards of thirty thousand children from the township and surrounding municipalities. Tracy also runs contests, hayrides, and a petting zoo. Each spring, the township's second and third graders plant squash seeds in their school and then bring the trays to the Farm Market for transplanting. When the squash are ready to be picked, the children delegate a team of classmates to bring in the harvest. "You know, we tell the children to bring their parents to see what they've planted," said Tracy. She smiled, because many of the parents then become customers of the Farm Market.

Most of the Duffield farm is now preserved through the state's preservation program, but the Duffield family would be in business for the long haul even if it hadn't been paid to stay in business. "We weren't looking to make money," said Duffield. "We enjoy what we're doing, and we wanted to stay here. I know we could have got a lot more money out of it than we did for preserving [the 170 acres], but that's all right. The whole family is involved with the farm, and it keeps everybody right here."

Why do the residents of Washington Township, the busy people, many of whom have moved there from urban areas, need the Duffield farm? Why should they care? Duffield has an answer:

> [They] can get all the fruits and vegetables almost the whole year-round now, and it's not like it used to be, but there's a much better taste and quality to fruits and vegetables that are raised locally and picked at the maturity they should be. A lot of the fruits and vegetables [grown elsewhere and sold in supermarkets] are picked when they're green and they're never very good. We pick our peaches tree-ripened, for example, and we've had so many people say how they can't believe the difference in the taste. They tell us they've bought peaches at the supermarket and they're blah. What we raise is picked and consumed the same day. That's the way it should be.

And farming is the way it's going to be for the Duffields. "I've been farming all my life," said Duffield, sitting at a table in a back room of the Farm Market, a John Deere hat on his head. "I'm a farmer. I never played any sports or anything in high school because we had to come home and work on the farm all the time. That's all I know is farming. When I got married, our children all seemed to love it, too. My wife does. We all enjoy what we're doing and enjoy being around people. We're not getting rich, but we're making a nice living. I think there's a need for us here."

It is impossible, of course, to say whether suburban sprawl would have obliterated so much farmland in New Jersey and elsewhere as rapidly and as overwhelmingly as it did after World War II had it not been for the GI Bill of Rights, but, as pointed out earlier in this chapter, it is true that many farmers in those postwar decades were unprepared for the kinds of capitalization, mechanization, and specialization required by the agricultural demands of the second half of the twentieth century. Many small farmers in particular, therefore, were vulnerable and easily convinced to sell out by realtors and developers.

In April 1973, the Blueprint Commission on the Future of New Jersey Agriculture issued a good-news–bad-news report after assessing the condition of farming in the Garden State in the wake of more than twenty years of unrelenting pressure from the forces of development. The good news was that most of New Jersey's remaining farmers were better managers than their forebears, their farms were larger, they invested more capital, mechanization replaced hand labor, and outdated methods were no longer practiced. Today's farmers make better use of their land and sources of water. They also plant and harvest what the markets are looking to buy.

The bad news was, in one sense, not news at all. Farming has always been a risky business, susceptible to disaster in any season as the result of bad weather or widely fluctuating prices and consumer demand. Nevertheless, the commission's report called attention to what it labeled as the "impermanence of agriculture." Most nonfarmers—consumers of farm products—drive to the roadside stand or supermarket and count on the produce they want being there in sufficient supply. In other words, we take for granted that farmers always will be working their fields because they know we need them. That assumption, the commission reminded us, may be in danger given current and future trends in the economy and the demand for more and more housing. Still another way to think of the impermanence of agriculture is that, in the end, we need farmers more than they need us.[18]

The blueprint the commission crafted pointed the way toward the creation of a "permanent land preserve for agricultural production" that would make it "feasible for farmers to farm this land and make a profit." Five years earlier, William H. Whyte, who at the time was editor of *Fortune* magazine and a Distinguished Professor at Hunter College, wrote a book that also outlined a kind of blueprint, one that called for drastic revisions in the assessment of farmland and bold new concepts for preservation. Most nonfarmers, conscientious conservationists included, want open land for esthetic reasons, Whyte argued. "Farmers are less prompted by esthetic concerns. If the area is a prime agricultural one, however . . . the leading farmers tend to share the gentry's attitude about the land, albeit for different reasons. They are mindful of the money they might eventually reap by selling out to a developer, but most of them really do want to continue farming. But the farmer has a price."[19]

The price that enlightened legislators and a generous public are now prepared to pay is simply to make it possible for farmers in the Garden State and across the country to continue at their most useful and necessary labor and to survive financially without turning over their precious land for houses, condos, and strip malls.

"Keep Farmers Farming" ❧ CHAPTER 4

In addition to house-hunting veterans and marginal farm families unable to or not choosing to adjust to the demands of postwar agribusiness, developers and realtors who looked upon farmland and saw four rooms and a bath out of one eye and dollar signs out of the other also had on their side in the 1950s and '60s land assessment policies that prevented many farmers from making a profit and made their green acres attractive and vulnerable to bulldozers.

Lacking a unified state policy regarding taxation in the first half of the twentieth century, county and municipal tax assessors based their property assessments on local ordinances and traditional practices. If borough or township law dictated that farmland should be assessed at the same rate as developed land, then so be it.[1]

A Rutgers University study in the late 1950s reported that farm real estate taxes in New Jersey "had increased at an annual average rate of 15 percent, with the result that New Jersey farmers were paying the highest real estate taxes of all farmers in the nation. By 1960, real estate taxes per capita for the New Jersey farm population were $360, but for the total population, the figure was only $138."[2]

Farmers were paying property taxes according to the residential or commercial development value of their land rather than on the basis of its productivity as farmland. To correct this punishing practice, the state legislature, at the urging of the New Jersey Farm Bureau, passed a law in 1962 that required tax assessors to assess farmland according to its agricultural productivity, rather than what its value would be if the farmland were sold to a developer who would put houses or a strip mall on the acreage. However, the law was challenged, and the state Supreme Court ruled that the statute was unconstitutional because the state constitution required all real property "to be assessed according to the same standard of value regardless of ownership."[3]

As a consequence of the court's ruling, Governor Richard J. Hughes appointed the Farmland Assessment Committee. The committee suggested an amendment to the state constitution that would permit farmland to be assessed at a rate different from that applied to residential and commercial property.

The Citizens Committee to Save Open Space then was formed by the New Jersey Farm Bureau and Grange to help convince New Jersey voters that farmland was worth saving and that the best way to accomplish this end was, first, to amend the state constitution and then to write a new law that would allow farmland to be assessed at a different rate from developed property. The committee secured the backing of many diverse groups representing business, education, environmental concerns, urban and suburban populations, and various other ethnic, political, and social segments of the Garden State.

The committee employed every means of securing public support it could conceive of: brochures, leaflets, inserts in utility bills and egg cartons, flyers delivered with milk (many dairies still delivered to homes then), news releases, paid ads in newspapers and on radio, and live appearances at events and on television. The committee's campaign in favor of a state constitutional amendment that would allow the legislature to pass a state taxation policy was very effective. For the first time, voters would have an opportunity to express how they felt about open space and "green acres," the terms used to appeal to the public.[4]

The proposed amendment went before the voters in November 1963 and passed by a vote of more than two to one. It is important to note that voters in the most urban counties valued open space as much as those in rural areas, perhaps more so since they enjoyed less of it. For example, the vote in Essex County—home to Newark—was 107,596 yes and 48,756 no, and in Hudson County across the river from Manhattan, the vote was 63,277 yes and 36,298 no. With the amendment in place, the legislature adopted the Farmland Assessment Act in 1964. To be eligible for a tax break under the law, farmland must consist of at least five acres, be "actively devoted" to agriculture, and be productive.

✳ *Farmers Fairly Taxed*

"The Farmland Assessment Act, by no stretch of the imagination, was the best and strongest piece of legislation New Jersey ever passed to protect farmland," according to Art Brown, former secretary of agriculture and the voice for Jersey Fresh during the tenure of Governor Christie Whitman. Sitting at the kitchen table in his farmhouse in Egg Harbor in the fall of 2003, Brown talked about farmland assessment and preservation. "[Under the 1964 law], the farmer didn't have to pay taxes at the development value. For example, today, if lots for development around here were selling for fifty thousand dollars and my farmland was assessed at the same value, I wouldn't be able to farm. I couldn't afford to." One of Brown's farm products is blueberries.

"New Jersey has the highest farmland taxes right now," said Brown. "Even with farmland assessment, we're number one in the country. So, you know, we have a lot going against [farmers] in New Jersey. Production costs are high, so we need as many benefit programs as we can possibly get if we're going to keep agriculture viable in the state. If we didn't have the Farmland Assessment Act, agriculture in New Jersey would have gone by the wayside a long time ago." According to the New Jersey Division of Taxation, the average value of an acre of farmland in New Jersey in 2002 was $9,245. That figure compared to $1,213 for the United States, $1,706 for New York State, $3,419 for Pennsylvania, and $3,526 for California.

The Farm Bureau believes the Farmland Assessment Act was the tourniquet that helped stanch the gush of farmland acres into acres of houses and strip malls that began post–World War II and continued up through 1970. Over the nearly twenty-year period from 1953 to 1970, 650,000 farm acres were lost, but in the thirty-year period after 1970, a little more than a third of that number—240,000 acres—disappeared.

🌺 Farmland Preservation Urged

Nine years after enactment of the Farmland Assessment Act, Governor William T. Cahill appointed the Blueprint Commission on the Future of New Jersey Agriculture. Perhaps the commission's most important contribution to the ongoing effort to stop the bleeding of productive farmland was its finding that an "impermanence syndrome" had infected New Jersey farmers, causing some to back off from investing in their agribusiness and leading them to make too many short-term and generally bad decisions about their farm's future.

No wonder farmers suffered from an "impermanence syndrome." Imagine you are a farmer who is barely making a profit, and you envision a future where your operational costs, such as the purchase and maintenance of equipment and the repair and replacement of farm buildings, will continue to go up while the price you can get for your products will either stay about the same or perhaps decline. So you ask yourself hard questions: Can I afford farming? What do I need to do to stay in business? What alternatives do I have? Should I get out of farming, sell my farm to a developer, and find work outside of agriculture?

The commission also was the first official body to conclude that farmland could best be preserved by government purchase of easements. However, the commission's recommendation was not converted into a viable program at the time, and, according to Art Brown, farmland preservation was placed on "the back burner." It pretty much stayed there for the remainder of the decade.

New Jersey got off the back burner on Halloween, 1980, when the state Department of Agriculture issued the results of a year-long study intended to chart "an agriculture retention and development program." The report became known simply as *Grassroots*. The commission concluded: "Those concerned with the preservation of agricultural land must recognize that the chief objective is to keep farmers farming by making sure that agriculture remains an economically and humanly attractive business."[5]

The commission's recommendations included a renewed call for the purchase of farmland easements. Another key suggestion was to enact right-to-farm legislation that would exempt farmers from nuisance ordinances and other regulations that were unrealistic and harmful to farming operations. *Grassroots* also recommended the creation of county and state agriculture development boards whose function would be to implement and monitor farmland retention techniques.[6]

🐾 Public Supports Preservation

Both public support and legislative action sprouted quickly from *Grassroots*, almost at the speed of light when one considers how long it normally takes for major statewide movements and political agendas to come to fruition. If farmers and legislators were pleasantly surprised in 1963 when voters authorized the first step toward farmland preservation by voting overwhelmingly for the amendment to the state constitution that made differential farmland assessment a reality, they must have been overjoyed when voters went to the polls in November 1981 and, again by a wide margin, approved the Farmland Preservation Bond Act that authorized the appropriation of $50 million to help slow down the dribbling away of the Garden State's gardens. The vote of 1981 was the first of several elections where the people of the nation's most urban state, many of whom live down the mean streets of cities or on cul-de-sacs where vegetables or fruit once ripened, resolutely decided that New Jersey's farm legacy, whose past and present history many were unaware of, was worth protecting.

The state legislature paid tribute to the people in a preamble to one of two first fruits of the *Grassroots* report, the Agriculture Retention and Development Act, adopted January 26, 1983: "The strengthening of the agricultural industry and the preservation of farmland are important to the present and future economy of the state and the welfare of the citizens of the state . . . and the people have demonstrated recognition of this fact through their approval of the Farmland Preservation Bond Act."

Governor Thomas Kean signed the Agriculture Retention and Development Act and the companion Right to Farm Act at the annual state agricultural convention held that year at the Cherry Hill Inn. Curiously, in view of the momentous impact those laws, particularly the former, were to have on the future fate of the Garden State, the *Philadelphia Inquirer* the next day made no mention of the laws in the headline that spanned page one of its New Jersey/Metro section, and in the article reporting the convention, the new laws did not get mentioned until the eighth paragraph, almost an afterthought: "The convention was a short one—a 2 1/2-hour affair during which several agriculturists were honored and two farm protection bills were signed into law by Gov. Kean."[7]

The Agriculture Retention and Development Act established the basic programs at the state and county levels, which, allowing for periodic refinements, are primarily responsible for preserving farmland in the Garden State. Most of the acreage is saved when county agriculture development boards approve and then recommend to the State Agriculture Development Committee (SADC) the purchase of easements that restrict those acres to farming forever. The farmer who is paid for easements on his land may sell his property or later will it to heirs, but the land, because of the deed restrictions, can never be used for residential or commercial development. According to Greg Romano, executive director of the SADC through 2004, the process for determining what farmland will be preserved through easements and at what cost to the municipality, county, and state (the state pays 60 to 80 percent of the purchase price) involves, first of course, willingness on the part of a farmer to participate in the program. Then, the selected land is appraised twice at the county level. The appraisers consider two land values. The first is its value as unrestricted land—that is, what the property might sell for development—and the second value is what it would be worth if the land were permanently restricted to farming. The appraisals are submitted to the SADC for review. Ordinarily, if approval is granted at the state level, said Romano, the county/state will pay the farmer the difference between the two figures.

In the fall of 2005, the SADC was considering changes to the preservation process that would, in the words of Agriculture

Secretary Charles M. Kuperus, "provide an alternative to our current county grants program in which we [the SADC] would approve funding not for individual farms, but for entire project areas identified by each county. By streamlining the administrative process, we could shorten the timeframe from application to preservation by six months or more." For example, a section of a county where the land is used almost exclusively for agriculture and may include a number of farms could be preserved as a unit, with individual farmers still reimbursed separately according to the acreage they own.

While the state program officially got off the ground in 1983, the Burlington County Board of Freeholders and a regional body called the Pinelands Environmental Council helped show the way six years earlier. In 1977, government officials and environmentalists living in Burlington and Ocean counties, which include most of the million-acre Pinelands, were becoming increasingly alarmed at the prospect that some enterprising residential or commercial developers could come along and grab up chunks of the environmentally sensitive but unprotected Pinelands and not only pollute the pure water aquifer that lies beneath the white sand, but also endanger the cranberry industry that flourishes in the bogs. They had a real scare in 1963 when an article appeared in the *New York Times* with the headline "Agency in Jersey Plans a New City." The article reported that the then-existing Pinelands Regional Planning Board was proposing to build a "new city that would ultimately offer 250,000 inhabitants 'the amenities sought after in the suburbs and a level of services found only in a large city.'" The heart of the proposed city on the outer skin of the pinelands would be a 240-acre convention center designed for shopping, offices, and entertainment. A heliport was proposed for each end of the center. Residents of the city would live in high-rise apartments. Presumably, persons living on the top floors would have an ocean view, albeit from a distance of twenty or so miles.

✷ *Easements Preserve Farmland*

In 1977, Robert C. Shinn was both a Burlington County freeholder and a member of the Pinelands Environmental Council (PEC). Shinn recently recalled that critical period for the Pinelands and how the PEC and the Burlington County Board of Freeholders initiated in New Jersey and in much of the country the concept of conservation easements. "It was clear that there were all kinds of pressures on the Pinelands and farmland. I got the idea for purchasing land easements [from the state's earlier Blueprint Commission], but I didn't know exactly how to go about it, because I didn't know of any county or state that was doing it then." Through contacts, he eventually heard that preservationists in Jackson Hole, Wyoming, who were intent on protecting open space in that scenic area, had purchased easements. "So we got information from them, and I came up with this plan for purchasing easements in the Pinelands." The next step was to find the money to pay for the easements. With the backing of his fellow Burlington County freeholders, Shinn drafted a resolution calling for a county referendum to approve a $1 million bond issue to cover the cost of the easements. Voters approved the bond issue by a three-to-one margin. "Our first purchase was easements on Fred Mahler's 530-acre cranberry farm. We paid him $238,500; I think that figures out to be about $450 an acre."

Under the Agriculture Retention and Development Act, the counties and state may also join forces to save farmland by purchasing it outright at fair market value, under the act's fee simple program, and then auctioning the land, again with the restriction against future development. The first such purchase in the state after passage of the act occurred in 1985 in Chesterfield Township, again in Burlington County. Shinn was a state assemblyman by that time. Wearing his new hat, he became the primary architect of the purchase that saved 608 acres of prime Burlington County farmland. Now a private consultant (the office is located in his stately Victorian home in Hainesport), Shinn explained how it all came about:

> A builder, Chesterfield Commons, owned the 608 acres, which included five tracts, and had plans for a 1,066-unit housing development. I talked to the builder and was told that they would sell the five farms for $3 million. I said there's no way we're going to be able to give you $3 million. [The "we" at this stage included three entities—the state, Burlington County, and Chesterfield

Township, none of whom were totally committed to the deal at the time of this meeting.] I told the builder that we had had the properties appraised at $1.6 million. The builder came back and said there was no way they would sell for that amount. So, I called another builder friend of mine, and he said he would talk to the builder of Chesterfield Commons. He later said he had told the builder of Chesterfield Commons, "Look, you don't want to incur the public's wrath by holding out for $3 million. You ought to try and take a reasonable profit and get out of it." My friend said Chesterfield Commons would settle for $2 million.

When I went to the [Burlington County] Board of Freeholders, they said they wouldn't spend $2 million [although they had raised that much through a bond issue] but would contribute $1.6 million, the figure that the land was appraised at. So, I went to Frank Wallace, then mayor of Chesterfield Township, and I told him that it was going to take $2 million to buy the farms, and I needed $400,000 from the township. Without batting an eye, the mayor said, "You've got it." He mentioned some timeframe that I thought was impossible, but, sure enough, a couple of weeks later a check came to the freeholders for $400,000. To this day, I don't know how they did it. Of course, I didn't question them. I had the money.

The farmland was finally purchased from Chesterfield Commons for $1.95 million, and an auction was scheduled for June 8, 1985. At 11 o'clock that morning, approximately three hundred persons crowded into the Chesterfield Fire Station. By the time the auctioneer laid down his gavel, the 608 acres had been sold to three bidders for a little over $1 million. Governor Kean was on hand to present the freeholders a check for $412,000, the state's share of the purchase price.

One of the successful bidders was Mark Ericson, a semiretired pilot then living in Robbinsville. He bought a 69.25-acre farm for $152,394 with the intention of growing primarily soybeans and corn. Eighteen years later, he recalled how he first discovered the productive farms of the Garden State: "I grew up in Iowa on a farm where we raised corn and livestock. When I went into the air force as a pilot, I was assigned to McGuire Air Force Base. Like most outsiders, I expected to come to New Jersey and find every-thing crowded—house upon house upon house. When I got off the turnpike at exit 7 and headed for the base, I was pleasantly sur-prised. I said to myself, 'Hey, this isn't going to be so bad after all.' "

In reporting the successful auction, the *Burlington County Times* called it a red-letter day for the Garden State's "fledgling farmland preservation program." Indeed it was, and the fledgling has been in full flight ever since. The number of farm acres pre-served in Burlington County alone since those 608 in June 1983 soared to 35,750 by the summer of 2004, placing the county among the top twelve counties in the nation with the best record in farmland preservation.

✦ *Preservation Effort Proves Successful*

The State Department of Agriculture boasted at the end of 2005 that more than 139,000 acres of farmland had been permanently protected against residential or commercial development in the state. Those figures meant that approximately 17 percent of avail-able farmland had been preserved, the highest percentage of any state.

Helping to attain that goal was the Warren County Department of Land Preservation, which began 2005 by preserving its hun-dredth farm and becoming one of only four counties among the twenty-one in New Jersey to reach that level. The county/state combination purchased a 161-acre farm for $966,216 ($6,000 an acre) with the intention of auctioning it after the example first established in Burlington County twenty-two years earlier. Joel Schnetzer, chairman of the county Agricultural Development Board, said at the time of the purchase of the hundredth farm that he could recall a summer day in the 1980s when his father, a farmer, upon hearing of the passage of the Agriculture Retention and Development Act, knocked on the door of every farmer's house in the county from Riegelsville on the Delaware River in the south to Hackettstown in the mountains up north to encourage farmers to attend a meeting at the Asbury Fire House. That gath-ering proved to be the start of the farmland preservation program in the county.

FIGURE 1. Seabrook Farms in Cumberland County was initially one of the major canneries in the state; then it became the first company in the world to produce frozen fruits and vegetables. Here, workers unload spinach (circa 1950). Frozen creamed spinach, now packaged by Seabrook Brothers & Sons, is the only product left that bears the original Seabrook Farms label. (Courtesy of the Seabrook Educational and Cultural Center.)

FIGURE 2. Signs of the times in the Garden State since the end of World War II. The sign on the near side of the street advertises new single-family homes, while the sign across the street, perhaps anticipating the spread of the development, offers another farm for sale. (Photo by author.)

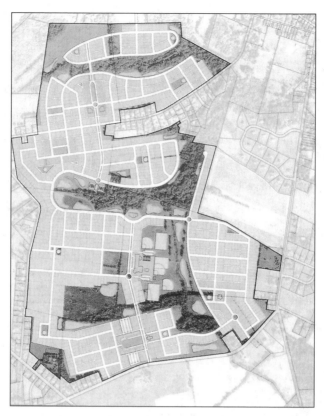

FIGURE 3. Chesterfield Township was the first municipality in New Jersey to come up with a plan to preserve farms by requiring developers to buy development rights, or credits, from farmers willing to preserve their farms and then to use those credits to build a mix of housing styles in a well-designed "receiving district," or town center, shown here. The state preservation program modeled after Chesterfield's Old York Village is called Transfer of Development Rights (TDR). (Courtesy of Clarke•Caton•Hintz.)

FIGURE 4. The firm Melvin/Kernan has conceived a TDR plan for Woolwich Township, Gloucester County. The receiving district is intended to save more than three thousand acres of farmland. The receiving district, which will contain no detached single-family dwellings, straddles old U.S. Route 322 west of the New Jersey Turnpike. (Courtesy of Melvin/Kernan.)

FIGURE 5. A worker for the Atlantic Blueberry Company carries her box of blueberries to a waiting truck. (Photo by author.)

FIGURE 6. Scott Walker shows some of the high-quality asparagus seeds developed by the Rutgers Agricultural Experiment Station in Bridgeton that his family business sells worldwide. (Photo by author.)

FIGURE 7. Organic farmer Jim Kinsel examines fresh produce that customers of his Community Supported Agricultural organic farm will choose for their weekly share of what Kinsel's Honey Brook Farms grows. (Photo by author.)

FIGURE 8. "Niche marketing" and "direct merchandising" have become primary goals for twenty-first-century farmers, and the Rutgers Food Innovation Center is showing the way. Santo Maccherone used to throw away overripe peaches because there was no market for them. Then, the Food Innovation Center helped him develop a new market: his own brand of Circle M Peach Cider Beverage. (Photo by author.)

FIGURE 9. The Duffields' family farm in Washington Township, Gloucester County, not only markets its produce in its own farm market, but the Duffields also teach children how to plant, grow, and harvest food—all about agriculture. It is not coincidental that the program for children attracts their parents as customers of the farm market. (Photo by author.)

FIGURE 10. Acquaculture is a multimillion-dollar business in the Garden State. The breeding and marketing of koi—ornamental fish—is a big part of the industry. The Quality Koi Company in Carneys Point, Salem County, is one of only six such farms in the country. Here, Mathew Mc-Cann, company manager, closes the net on koi about to be transferred to a holding tank, where the fish may be viewed by prospective buyers. (Photo by author.)

FIGURE 11. High-tunnel farming, not yet widely practiced in New Jersey, will likely be adopted by more farmers who see the tunnels as a way of prolonging the growing season for certain fruits and vegetables. Shirley Kline now grows raspberries in this high tunnel from April to Thanksgiving, an extension of three months to the usual growing season. (Photo by author.)

FIGURE 12. C. Reed Funk examines one of the thousands of nut trees he has planted in New Brunswick and Adelphia, Monmouth County. He argues for a "new Green Revolution" in which nut trees will be used to help feed the world's hungry. (Photo by author.)

Warren County is bordered by the Delaware River in the west and the Musconetcong River in the east; county road 519, which traverses Scotts and Jenny Jump Mountains, is one of a very few highways in New Jersey designated a scenic route, and, looking fifteen miles north out the window of Robert Resker's office on a clear day, one could see the mountain pass that is the Delaware Water Gap. Resker is director of the county's land preservation program. The visitor to his office is tempted to ask why, in this land of mountain resorts and fertile valleys, he and the County Agricultural Development Board should be concerned that developers might grab up farmland. Resker is also mayor of Allamuchy Township, which straddles Interstate 80, and he estimates that his municipality alone has preserved more farmland—some of the richest in the county—than almost any other community in the state. He has an answer to the visitor's question: "I can drive east on Interstate 80 to built-up Wayne in Passaic County in twenty-five minutes, and I can be crossing the George Washington Bridge into New York City in less than an hour. People and industry are moving west. They're coming our way."

Among the twenty-one counties, Warren ranks first in corn grown for grain, second in livestock and dairy cows, third in hay, tied for third in head lettuce, and fourth in soybeans. The county is doing whatever it can to accelerate farmland preservation, Resker said when interviewed at the start of 2005. "As of this date, we've preserved 12,500 acres. Our goals are 15,000 acres by 2006 and 20,000 by 2009." No one in Warren County or in Trenton would be surprised if the goals are achieved ahead of schedule.

✿ Preservation Benefits All New Jerseyans

Kuperus also points out that farmland preservation is a win-win situation for farmers and the citizens of the Garden State. When the state/county combination purchases farmland easements, for example, the farmer continues to own the land and frequently reinvests the money he receives to improve farm operations, to retire debt, or to buy more farmland. In a column he wrote for publication in New Jersey newspapers, Kuperus stated that the owner of a preserved farm "continues to pay taxes but [his farm] requires little in the way of municipal services. A preserved farm does not trigger the construction of a new school. A preserved farm does not require annual spending for [school] staff and maintenance." A study by the American Farmland Trust reported that for every dollar a municipality collects in tax revenue from a farm, the municipality expends thirty-six cents in services to the farm. In contrast, for every dollar collected from residential property, the local government must spend a dollar and fifteen cents for services. Finally, Kuperus stated, "Agriculture provides a homegrown food supply that is fresh, dependable, affordable, and safe."

✱ *Citizens Support Preservation Financing*

Earlier, mention was made of the generosity of New Jersey citizens as demonstrated by their support of major funding proposals that finance farmland preservation. In 1998, voters approved an amendment to the state constitution that established a billion-dollar Garden State Preservation Trust that dedicates a portion of the annual sales tax revenue to the preservation of farmland, open space, and historic places. That portion amounts to about $87 million a year, with the greatest share of the funds going to save farmland. Voters further authorized the state to borrow another billion dollars over the ten-year period ending in 2008.

As previously noted, the state legislature passed the Right to Farm Act on the same date in 1983 when it adopted the Agriculture Retention and Development Act. The act became necessary as suburbia sprawled and bumped into rural reality. Some families who, when loading up the moving van, had talked enthusiastically about heading into the country and delighting in the fragrance of fields of tasseled corn and orchards of peach blossoms, became disenchanted and then bothersome when the odors turned out to be pesticides and piles of rotting apples.

The Right to Farm Act is intended to protect "commercial farm operations from nuisance action [including restrictive municipal ordinances] where recognized methods and techniques of agricultural production are applied." The "recognized methods and techniques" include the following: processing and packaging agricultural products, operating a farm market, replenishing "soil nutrients" (read spreading smelly fertilizer), controlling plant and animal pests and diseases, clearing woodlands and open burning of brush, and "on-site disposal of organic agricultural wastes" (e.g., rotting apples). In other words, a farm is a farm is a farm.

"Visualize a strip of land half a mile wide stretching from New York to California. That is one million acres—the amount of important farmland converted to other uses and irreversibly lost to agriculture every year in the United States." That is the scary preamble to a federal document published in 1981, the year after New Jersey's *Grassroots* first gave direction to the state's program for agriculture retention and development. The federal document that roused the nation continued:

> Citizens across the country and their representatives at all levels of government have shared rapidly deepening concerns over the adverse effects of this loss of agricultural land. Some feared the decline of rural life. . . . Others emphasized the economic disruption that accompanies the decline of agriculture in an area. Still others were apprehensive that continued loss of farmland would lead to reduced production that, in turn, would have grave impacts on the nation's ability both to feed itself and to make sufficient foreign sales that earn foreign exchange. Underlying these concerns is the realization that good farmland is a finite resource which is necessary for survival.[8]

The document became a blueprint of sorts for the federal Farm Bill of 1981, which turned out to be a well-intentioned but essentially toothless legislation whose apparent sole value was to call attention to problems without prescribing any specific or helpful solutions. One summary of the bill claimed the law simply required the federal government to evaluate those agricultural initiatives it funded.

✻ Federal Government Assumes Role

The federal government did not return to the issue of farmland preservation in any meaningful and helpful fashion until 1996 with passage of the Agricultural Improvement and Reform Act, which established the ongoing Farmland Protection Program. At the outset, the program's very modest goal for the period 1996–2001 was to help protect between 170,000 and 340,000 acres of farmland nationwide by providing matching funds to state and local governments who were preserving farmland through the purchase of easements. The law initially authorized the expenditure of $35 million for this purpose; an additional $50 million was later appropriated to aid in the protection of another 107,000 acres. As the 1996 act phased out, Congress passed the 2002 Farm Act. This law authorizes the Natural Resources Conservation Service of the U.S. Department of Agriculture to dole out, on average, $100 million a year in matching grants through 2007. It's a piddling amount when one considers that the state of New Jersey alone is spending almost that amount annually for farmland and open space preservation, and county and municipal governments are spending additional millions.

🌸 *TDR Becomes Successful Alternative*

Arguably the best way to protect farmland and preserve the Garden State's farming legacy into the future is a program that, at the same time, satisfies preservationists, farmers, and developers, and which costs taxpayers next to nothing. Unfortunately, because the program can be complicated and difficult to implement, many municipalities and counties are discouraged from even considering it. Also, for much of New Jersey, it may already be too late to make the program work. The program is called Transfer of Development Rights (TDR). It was officially adopted by the state in 2004 as one method of farmland preservation, but the state continues to promote and fund almost exclusively conservation easement and fee simple purchases authorized by the Agriculture Retention and Development Act of 1983.

This is how TDR works to preserve farmland: A municipal or county government establishes a sending area and a receiving area. The sending area consists of those farm acres that the municipality or county wishes to preserve. The receiving area is a section of the municipality or county that has been set aside specifically for development. This development may include a variety of housing: single-family houses of varying sizes, townhouses, and other kinds of multiple-family dwellings. A developer purchases development rights, or credits, from owners of farmland in the sending area who have agreed to preserve their farms forever through deed restrictions (they continue to own the land). The number of allotted credits an owner of farmland can sell to a developer is based on a formula established by the municipality or county, a calculation that takes into consideration, for example, the quality of soil and how the farmland is used. The developer then can use the credits he has bought from a landowner to purchase acreage in the designated receiving area.

TDR works best when a municipality or county government is able to separate land already developed from undeveloped farmland. The municipality or county can then create distinct sending and receiving zones. If local or county governments have allowed housing developments to be scattered across the land, it becomes almost impossible to set aside these two zones. Of course, TDR does not work in those communities where developers have no interest in purchasing development rights from farmers because there is no incentive or apparent demand for housing in the area. To date, TDRs have not worked well in rural areas where, for whatever reason, people have evidenced no desire to live and, consequently, there is no pressure from developers to gobble up farmland.[9]

TDR is not a radical twenty-first century concept. Hundreds of counties and municipalities across the country have authorized TDR programs over the last two decades; however, not very many have put the programs into practice. A primary reason why active TDR programs are few in number is because they can be difficult and costly to establish. To begin with, the county or municipality must be able to designate sending and receiving districts that include enough land, usually in the hundreds of acres, to make the program worthwhile. Another obstacle to establishing TDR in rural areas is the necessity of creating a sewerage system for the receiving district.

Despite the challenges, a number of communities continue to consider TDR as a possible method—perhaps the best method—to preserve farmland on a large scale. They site these considerations: designated sending and receiving districts help manage and control population growth; developers buy farmland easements rather than governments using taxpayers' money; not only do farmers benefit, but open space also is preserved for the public benefit.[10]

Montgomery County, Maryland, which had the distinction in 2004 of being number one in farmland preservation among all counties in the United States, relies primarily on its TDR program. For example, of 61,394 acres preserved through August 2004, considerably more than half were protected through the county's TDR program. Many persons find Montgomery County's standing in the nation and this statistic (the county's preservation goal is 70,000 acres) to be astounding bordering on the unbelievable. Montgomery County is to the nation's capital, for example, what Bergen County is to New York City and Camden County is to Philadelphia—next door. For Montgomery County, its proximity to Washington has meant not only that its communities must build bedrooms for thousands of commuters into the city, but the county has become home to dozens of industries, particularly as they line up on either side of Interstate 270. "Farms may not be what most people envision when they think of Montgomery County," stated a news release from the county government announcing its number one status, "[but] Montgomery County has a long and rich agricultural heritage that has helped raise the quality of life for every resident. What many people may not be aware of . . . is that Montgomery County continues to have a thriving agricultural industry that contributes more than $251 million to the local economy."

And what most Americans and probably most New Jersey residents don't know is that in this, the most densely populated state of the fifty, the food and agricultural complex pumps more than $63 billion into the state's economy each year.

While New Jersey authorized TDR as a means of farmland preservation for the entire state in 2004, to date its implementation has been limited to the Pinelands and Chesterfield Township in Burlington County, both jurisdictions having initiated the process long before the state government got around to making it available statewide. TDR has proved to be successful in both places, but, particularly in Chesterfield Township, success has not come easily or quickly.

New Jersey created the Pinelands Commission in 1979 soon after the Congress ruled that the Pinelands required protection from development that might destroy one of the most ecologically unique places on the East Coast (the Pinelands have since been declared an International Biosphere Reserve by the United Nations). Two years later, in 1981, the commission drafted a plan that included a preservation area and a designated growth area on the fringes of the Pinelands; the growth area is composed of twenty-four municipalities. The commission helped the municipalities design master plans and zoning ordinances that identify receiving areas within their boundaries where developers may use development rights or credits they purchase from landowners in the Pinelands to build houses, according to Susan Grogan, spokesperson for the Pinelands Commission.

The commission allocates to landowners in the preservation area one development right for approximately nine acres. The exact equivalency depends on the quality of the acreage and whether it is upland, woodland, wetlands, or farmland. A developer needs one development right to build one house. Sales of development rights are strictly private business transactions between landowners and developers. In 2005, said Grogan, landowners were selling a development right for an average price of $30,000. Nine years ago, a right sold for $4,000 or $5,000. In 1985, the state created the Pinelands Development Credit Bank. This act allowed the Credit Bank, which is a separate entity from the Pinelands Commission, to accept and store development rights from landowners as credits (four rights equal one credit) and make interested developers aware of them. However, final sales of credits or rights are still concluded between buyer and seller. On one or two occasions in the past, Grogan said, the Credit Bank has held a credit auction.

As of January 2005, the Pinelands Commission, through its TDR program, had preserved 42,800 acres of the Pinelands. Approximately 24,000 of those acres were classified as farmland, which included cranberry bogs and farms planted in vegetables, grains, or fruits.

That portion of Old York Road where Mr. and Mrs. Larry Durr live doubles as a kind of dam holding back sprawl. North and west of the road and just behind the fence in the Durrs' backyard is a huge reservoir of housing, mostly townhouses, in Bordentown Township. South and east of the road, across from the Durrs' rancher, is open space—farmland—in Chesterfield Township. The Durrs live in Chesterfield Township, and, in the year 2005, Durr was mayor (he has been on the Township Committee since 1990). Today, Durr talks proudly about Chesterfield's TDR program; a dozen years ago he campaigned against it.

The reasons for his earlier opposition pretty much parallel the obstacles previously cited: the considerable and careful advance planning and coordination required, and the need to build an infrastructure capable of supporting the development of the receiving district. "We had a lot of hot meetings. Most of us, including me, were not opposed to TDR as a concept. However, at the time, we couldn't agree on the sending and receiving areas. Also, the township had no sewerage system to accommodate housing in the receiving area, and I, for one, saw no chance of the township being able to afford one."

Enter Robert Shinn—yes, the same Robert Shinn who was first to come to the rescue of the Pinelands and who was then among the first to implement the programs later established by the Agriculture Retention and Development Act. Then, in the 1990s, and wearing a new hat as head of the state Department of Environmental Protection, Shinn saw a way to help Chesterfield advance a TDR program. "I knew the commissioner for corrections pretty well, so I talked to him and . . ." What happened next was the commissioner of corrections agreed to a plan whereby Chesterfield could establish a receiving area in the northwest section of the township not far from the Albert C. Wagner Correctional Institution (located in Chesterfield) and then tie into the institution's sewerage treatment plant. The township had to pay for an expansion of the institution's treatment plant to accommodate the planned development, but Shinn arranged for a low-interest loan from the state to cover that cost.

With one of the major obstacles overcome, the Township Planning Board and later the Township Committee, in 1998, adopted a new master plan and strategy for implementing a TDR program. The plan called for creation of a 560-acre receiving area called Old York Village located near the Village of Crosswicks in the township, a tiny settlement that dates to 1677. The father of Richard Stockton, who was one of New Jersey's signers of the Declaration of Independence, owned property not far distant. According to the brochure developed by the township, Old York Village provides for over twelve hundred housing units in a variety of attached and detached single family housing types that include the township's "fair share of housing affordable to low and moderate income households," a new elementary school adjacent to centralized active recreation facilities, a network of neighborhood parks, a mixed-use village center with retail, office, and convenience uses to serve local market needs, and preserved stream corridors with walking paths that will connect the respective neighborhoods and extend north to Crosswicks Village.

In Chesterfield Township, the interests of landowners, farmers, homebuilders, and open space preservationists have all been considered. Each house built in Old York Village represents the retirement of a development credit and the preservation of farmland in the balance of the township—the sending district. Much like the historic settlements of Crosswicks, Chesterfield, and Sykesville, the new village—the receiving district—also will be surrounded by the prosperous farms of Chesterfield Township.

Toll Brothers, Inc., of Pennsylvania was the first developer to build houses in Old York Village. By spring of 2005, Toll Brothers had sold thirty of thirty-six planned estate homes at a beginning price in the "low $600,000s" and had sold 25 of an additional 144 single-family dwellings envisioned by Toll Brothers for its Old York Village section called Chesterfield Greene. Early in 2005, the price of most of these other planned houses ranged from approximately $390,000 up to $450,000. "There are some advantages and disadvantages to being part of [a TDR program]," said Michael Assofsky, manager for Chesterfield Greene. "An advantage is that [TDR] eliminates our cost of having to research property that we might be interested in buying. A disadvantage is that the approval process is more [time consuming and] expensive for us, and, of course, that adds to the cost of construction. [TDR] is neither good nor bad for us, really; it's a trade-off."

Max Spann, Jr., of Max Spann Auction Company of Clinton believes TDR is more good than bad for developers. He came to that conclusion in the summer of 2004 when he conducted the first-ever auction of development rights, or credits, to be held by a county or municipality in New Jersey. The auction took place on a hot night in the Chesterfield fire hall. According to Larry Durr, the Township Committee hit on the idea of an auction because the sale of development credits by township landowners to developers had been in a slump and because the Township Committee was afraid that Burlington County, which has been building a bank of TDRs from municipalities that have no program of their own, might sell some of those credits to developers of Old York Village, thereby diminishing the chances of local landowners to sell their credits. "We told our landowners who had credits to sell that this was their chance," said Durr.

One of the reasons that sales of credits had slumped earlier, according to Spann, was that some landowners simply didn't know how many credits they had, while others were aware of their credits but had no idea how much to ask for them or how to contact interested developers. "Don't forget," said Spann, "a landowner with credits doesn't put a for sale sign on his property announcing how many credits he has. Selling credits is a very private negotiation." The primary advantage to the developer, according to Spann, is that, when the company buys credits at auction, there is only one contract for the company's attorney to peruse and sign off on. On the other hand, Spann argued, if the developer had to negotiate separately with each landowner and pay its attorney to settle each contract separately, the cost to the developer would be far greater.

At the 2004 auction, three developers were present: American Properties, Matzel & Mumford (a wholly owned subsidiary of K. Hovnanian), and Toll Brothers. The dozen or so sellers had indicated to Spann in advance of the auction the minimum price per credit they would accept. Spann conducted one round of bidding, and the highest bid, from Matzel & Mumford, was $50,000 per credit ($52,500 with fees). This amount was double what most credits had been sold for in the past. The company purchased fifty-seven credits at that price. The only sellers who were not happy with the results were a few who had indicated in advance they would only accept an amount that turned out to be much higher than the final bid price.

John Calabrese sold one credit at the auction, the last of six and three quarters credits he had when the TDR program first came into being. He sold the other five and three quarters to Matzel & Mumford at an earlier date, and for less than $50,000 per credit. Indeed, Calabrese feels sorry for those landowners who sold credits at the beginning of the TDR program and received $25,000 or much less per credit. Of course, one expects the value of land to increase through the years, but Calabrese's empathy for other landowners illustrates one of the problems mentioned by Max Spann: landowners often are unaware of what credits they have— or should have—and often they have no way of knowing how much a credit is worth on the open market.

Calabrese owns approximately twenty-three acres on Sykesville-Wrightstown Road, where he raises standard-bred horses, most of which spend their life in harness racing at the Meadowlands or Freehold racetracks; sometimes, he drives the sulky himself. He also keeps horses that "need a vacation" from the racetracks. Calabrese came to Chesterfield Township in 1988 from North Arlington in Bergen County. "I've liked horses since I was a kid. During summers when I was in college, I worked at the Giants' Stadium in the Meadowlands, which is nearby the racetrack, and eventually I got over to the track and . . . well, I decided I wanted to move out of North Jersey and own a horse farm."

When Calabrese looks over his acreage now, he sometimes envisions how the land might have been developed if Chesterfield Township, like so many other communities, permitted developments to be plunked down here, there, and everywhere. "A developer would probably divide my land in half with a street and then put up houses on either side. [Instead], my farm and all the land around me is preserved. It's great for me, and I think it's great for the township."

Chesterfield Township, which held off sprawl creeping down from up north and prevented housing developments to be scattered among the farmland like so many splotches, seems well satisfied with its TDR program. It preserves farmland while still allowing for controlled development and population growth. The only part of the plan that took township officials so long to put together that has yet to be realized is the new elementary school to be located in Old York Village. Voters in 2004 turned down a referendum that would have authorized construction of the school. The township currently has one K–6 school; older children attend a regional middle and senior high school.

Michele Byers, executive director of the New Jersey Conservation Foundation, is one of those who is convinced that TDR may be the best way to preserve what remains of farmland and open space in the Garden State, but she hopes the state did not wait too long to promote the program. "Many of us working to stem the tide of sprawl have pushed for TDR for almost twenty years!" she stated. "Just think what New Jersey might look like now if we had had the right tool thirty years ago. But even now, there is still much left to protect and many communities to benefit from TDR. TDR as a tool is not perfect, nor is it a panacea for all towns. It will take lots of work to tailor the program to meet local needs, and to do the required advance planning. But a little hard work is a small price to pay for towns that really want control of their growth and future destiny."[11]

✻ *Preserved Land Now Has Commercial Value*

As the year 2006 began, the state legislature passed a measure backed by the New Jersey Farm Bureau that allows minimal non-agricultural use of existing buildings on preserved farmland and very restricted construction of a building used for nonagricultural purposes. The reason for the amendment to existing preservation law, according to Ed Wengryn, Farm Bureau field representative and liaison between the bureau and the legislature, is to permit owners of preserved land to generate additional income without endangering or circumventing the preserved status of the land.

For example, Wengryn said, the amended law permits the owner of preserved farmland to sell space on a silo for a communications cell tower. The owner also could rent out an unused farm building for a commercial use, such as an antiques store. He cited a farmer who owns a large, vacant farm building on his preserved farm that he would like to use for a boat repair business. The new measure also permits the owner of preserved farmland to construct a building for commercial use that measures no larger than five hundred square feet. Such a building could be used as a small store, perhaps a woodworking shop, or a business office, said Wengryn.

All requests to use existing farm buildings for nonagricultural purposes or to construct new facilities must be approved by the State Agricultural Development Council and the governing body of the municipality from which a request originates.

Wengryn acknowledged that critics of the amended law view the measure as a slippery slope that eventually could lead to preserved land becoming unpreserved. Indeed, he said, some owners of preserved farmland have sought to "buy back" the land, that is, to reimburse state and county governments for whatever amount they originally paid the owners to preserve the land. "We are firmly against 'buy back,'" said Wengryn. "This measure simply allows farmers to generate some additional income without jeopardizing the preserved farmland. We're happy with that."

"We Sure Hope 🌿 CHAPTER 5
It Works"

A s we enter the second half of the first decade of the twenty-
first century, New Jersey residents from Cape May to Sussex
question whether the Garden State can sustain the early pace and
scope of farmland preservation and, at the same time, create and
maintain a delicate balance between farmers farming and developers developing.

The answers are hedged. To begin with, the state's ten-year
bankroll for farmland preservation ($129 million for fiscal 2005)
will run out in fiscal year 2009 (beginning July 1, 2008). No one, of
course, can give assurances that the fund for preservation, which
now is dependent on sales tax revenue dedicated for that purpose
by the legislature and bond issues, will be restocked at all, let alone
in that amount or any amount close to it. Perhaps thinking ahead
to the projected cutoff in fiscal year 2009, Susan Craft, when she
was director of Burlington County's preservation program in 2004,
told a newspaper reporter, "We have to lock down everything we
want to lock down in five years, or it will be spoken for." Craft was
named executive director of the state's Farmland Preservation Program in 2005.

Another hedge results from New Jersey's Municipal Land Use
law, which allows each of New Jersey's 566 municipalities to conceive its own master plan and decide how the land inside its borders

will be zoned. It may come as a surprise to learn that the zoning maps in nearly all of those municipalities do not now and never have set aside any land for purely agricultural purposes. In almost all cases existing farmland is zoned for development—always has been. In the past, farmland was likely zoned R-1 or R-2, which meant that rural (read farm) land could be divided into one- or two-acre building lots. Now, despite all of the state's considerable and ongoing attempts to conceive and enforce a smart growth land-use plan and accompanying map, "it's extremely difficult, if not impossible, to implement such a plan in a home rule state like New Jersey," claims Joanne Harkins, director of land use and planning for the New Jersey Builders Association. "Municipal compliance with [the map] is voluntary. Even in the so-called growth areas designated by the map, municipalities don't have to accept any growth. And they can downzone if they want to."

🥀 *Downzoning Is a Poor Preservation Tool*

Downzoning is the oxymoron that refers to a municipality's decision to *up* the size of a building lot. For example, a municipality that has zoned one- and two-acre building lots for decades may increase the lot size to five or more acres. That is called downzoning. Most preservationists agree that downzoning is not helpful. "Downzoning is actually sprawl inducing," argues Hawkins. "It's the exact opposite of what [everybody says] they want to have happen. It just spreads everything out over more and more land."

Paul M. Drake, planning director for both the state's Office of Smart Growth and Office of State Planning, concurs and also points to a sometimes overlooked consequence of downzoning. Under the terms of the Farmland Assessment Act adopted forty years ago to give farmers relief from property tax rates applied to land open to development or already developed, someone who owns at least five acres "actively devoted" to agriculture and earns at least $500 from those acres qualifies for the tax break. Where downzoning has created building lots in excess of six acres, Drake argues, the homeowner who buys one of those over-sized lots and builds his mansion on one acre of the lot can convert the remaining five acres into a "hobby farm" and qualify for the tax break. Drake describes how two owners of adjoining hobby farms that grow and harvest trees for sale might agree to take advantage of the law and deprive the municipality where they live of lawful and needed tax revenue: "'I sell you [a certain number of] cords of firewood and you sell me [a number of] cords back. I write you a check and you write me a check.' Five hundred dollars is not too much to swallow if you're going to save $6,000 on your taxes."

Other nonfarmers living on six-plus-acre lots also may avoid paying their fair property tax by raising just enough sheep or horses or soybeans on just enough acres and making just enough money. Michele S. Byers, executive director of the New Jersey Conservation Foundation, claims developers also can circumvent the Farmland Assessment Act. "Let's say a developer buys a farm with the intention of building a housing development, office complex or shopping mall. The new owner may hold the land for years waiting for it to increase in value. During this time, some trees are planted or cut, or hay is grown and baled, or cows are grazed, and the nonfarmer receives a substantial property tax break."[1]

At the end of 2004, the New Jersey Farm Bureau published the results of what it termed the "first systematic statewide study of the economic impact of downzoning on New Jersey's farmland owners." Clarion/Samuels Associates of Philadelphia, which conducted the study, concluded that downzoning, instead of benefiting everyone, as many municipalities that have instituted it claim, actually benefits no one, especially farmers. Richard Nieuwenhuis, Farm Bureau president, complained, "A municipality [by downzoning] can effectually reduce the value of the farm's fundamental financial assets by 17 to 77 percent. Downzoning can be the last straw for a farmer struggling against low prices and capricious weather." Nieuwenhuis called a municipality's decision to downzone a "vote of no confidence" in the farmers of that municipality.

According to Paul Drake, most municipalities that engage in downzoning claim that their action is designed to preserve farmland and open space or to protect the quality of life. "In my view, all of these [reasons] are a smoke screen. The hidden agenda is that [those municipalities] don't want more schoolchildren." Donald Matthews, who devoted twenty-one years to the governing body and planning board in Montgomery Township, Somerset County, admitted that holding the line on school enrollment was the principal reason why his planning board created five-acre building lots out of some of the best farmland in the township.

Even as downzoning does not preserve farmland and discriminates against the farmer, it also discriminates against the average family. According to the Builders League of South Jersey, the median sales price of a new home in the state increased from $190,000 in 1997 to nearly $383,000 in 2004. "It's no surprise that the average working family in New Jersey, earning approximately $55,000 annually, struggles to put a roof over its head," stated the League. None but the very wealthiest can afford to own the twenty-first-century castles built on five and ten-acre lots, Drake says, and if they have school-age children, they probably send them to a pricey private school. "The sad part is what we have done to families in New Jersey. There's no place for an average middle-income family, or a lower- or moderate-income family, to live in New Jersey."

Some planners advocate getting rid of all local zoning ordinances and maps, heaping on them, as they do, most of the blame for suburban sprawl. Journalist James Howard Kunstler argues that the primary fault of the typical zoning ordinance and master plan is that they unnaturally compartmentalize different living arrangements and commercial space. For example, the typical ordinance or plan may ensure that a zone or section of the community designed for families who can afford a medium-priced house is purposely but artificially separated from a zone intended for big houses for people with very big incomes. Furthermore, land set aside for parks and businesses is often zoned so distant from the families who desire and need the parks and businesses, that they must travel by car to reach them, which, of course, then necessitates constructing roads that further separate the community into scattered and disassociated fragments. The result of this kind of planning (if it can be called such), according to Kunstler, is a "formless, soulless, centerless, demoralizing mess."[2]

🔥 Municipalities Turn to Professional Planners

Given massive state funding for farmland preservation that is due to expire in a few years and dozens of outdated county and municipal master plans that don't protect farmland and may even penalize farmers and most home-seeking families, what does the future hold for farmland preservation?

The future of farmland preservation is perhaps less in the hands of those who plant and reap and more in the hands of those who plan and design, men and women with such unfamiliar initials after their name as PP (Professional Planner), AICP (American Institute of Certified Planners), and CNU (Congress for New Urbanism). People like Paul Drake, a member of AICP, who laments that it took "fifty years to mess up" the Garden State with poorly conceived development and who knows that the state may have only a few years remaining to save what's left of farmland in the wake of the post–World War II tsunami that drowned the landscape in disconnected single family housing developments, strip malls, and a network of congested highways.

Today's planning professionals initially spend much of their time correcting, updating, and replacing municipal master plans and zoning ordinances that aided and abetted the tsunami and which now, in the light of the first decade of the twenty-first century, are frightening to governing bodies and planning boards facing the prospect of massive and seemingly uncontrollable development and the swallowing up of remaining farmland and other open spaces. Sometimes—perhaps oftentimes—in the past, local officials sacrificed good land, the best farmland, in their desire and haste to bring in more ratables: oversized houses containing as few children as possible, small businesses, and light industry—anything that would help keep local property taxes in line. William H. Whyte, writing in the mid-sixties while many municipalities were being inundated with reckless development and before most had engaged professional planners to make sense of what was happening to their community, referred to their shortsightedness that had long-range consequences: "The members of the village and township boards are sympathetic toward the farmers . . . but what preoccupies them is the possibility of development, and they are not too choosy as to what kind. They are, in fact, pushovers for any entrepreneur who promises to increase the local tax base. In most cases they are quite unrealistic in their expectations."[3]

Increasingly, governments at all levels are looking to the professional planners and designers to come up with schemes that will, in fact, keep farmers farming and, at the same time, allow developers to develop—but sensibly. What many of the professionals envision are some combination of Transfer of Development Rights (TDR), which already has proven its worth in Burlington County and in other states, and Traditional Neighborhood Development (TND) or the New Urbanism, which also has been successful elsewhere. One important reason why both of these movements could be successful in preserving farmland while at the same time creating new living space for average families and new businesses is because neither requires huge outlays of tax revenue or government bond issues. Whereas farmland preservation up until now in the Garden State has depended primarily on the use of public funds to purchase development easements on privately owned farmland, TDR, as previously noted, requires developers to purchase such easements from farmers in the form of development rights or credits that are then used by the developers to build in designated receiving districts.

Another important reason why TDR and TND might be the keys to continued farmland preservation is because farmers may stand to earn more by selling easement rights to developers, who pass on that cost to home buyers and retailers, than by accepting what local, county, and state governments can afford to pay for the easements.

The traditional neighborhood of TND is like the town your great-grandparents were raised in but is now usually re-created with aluminum siding. It is intended to counter or replace the kind of twentieth-century development that plowed up farmland as fast as Caterpillars could move it and then created huge splotches of single-family dwellings often detached from one another and from those businesses and public facilities intended to serve them. The new urbanists scoff at developers who ruin a good piece of farmland with a splotch of houses that has no relationship to its surroundings. For example, a recently built South Jersey development of single-family houses is called Village Grande, but it is not a village by any true definition of that word, because there is no store, no school, no park, no church—no traditional element of a village—for several miles in any direction.

Among the primary proponents and practitioners of TND are Andrew Duany and Elizabeth Plater-Zyberg, whose Florida-based firm has designed more than two hundred new communities that feature what they and others call traditional neighborhoods. The hallmark of these communities is a town center where modest single-family dwellings, duplexes, townhouses, and other forms of multifamily housing are mixed together, and families, in most cases, are able walk to stores, parks, and schools. Indeed, the centers are often described as walkable as opposed to the typical drivable twentieth-century suburb. The reason TND is often referred to as New Urbanism is because the design is more urban than suburban, with housing of all kinds in close proximity as opposed to single-family houses sitting on one-, two-, or more-acre lots. However, open space, trees, gardens, picket fences, and those amenities that may be seen in the best suburbs are also incorporated into the new traditional neighborhoods.

🌸 Creating Town Centers

According to Duany and Plater-Zyberg, the traditional neighborhood—with a town center—should first depart from the typical suburban spread by requiring developers to place garages behind housing, perhaps on a shared alley or lane, instead of allowing them to eat up and dominate frontage. They also are strong advocates for bringing back front porches, which apparently were considered unnecessary when houses became air-conditioned, and picket fences. In their book about old sprawl and new design, the couple points to a TND their firm created in northern Virginia. Three developers were active in the area: two were small and local, the third was a huge, national conglomerate. The local developers went for the hidden garage, front porch, and picket fence, while the national firm stuck to the more typical suburban design. "After eighteen months on the market," the couple reported, "sales figures were as follows: Local Builder A: 30 homes; Local Builder B: 14 homes; Gorilla: 1 home. There was little interest in the conventional product when buyers were presented with equal access to its alternative."[4]

TND may complement TDR, but it also may be part of a different strategy. For example, a developer may buy farmland and agree to preserve a significant portion of it as farmland while creating a mixed-use village or hamlet on the remainder. The planning-architectural firm Clarke•Caton•Hintz, which, in 2005, had its office in the renovated West Trenton Railroad Station, has proposed just such a scheme to municipal officials in Delaware Township in farm-rich western Hunterdon County. Actually, the firm has placed on the township's planning board table three possible plans for developing a 120-acre farm now owned by a developer and leased to an area farmer. Plan One calls for a conventional subdivision that divides the property into thirty-six building lots of 3 acres each (some of the land is in woods) and leaves zero farmland or open space. Plan Two, labeled a cluster subdivision, also includes thirty-six lots, but each lot is 1.5 acres, leaving approximately 50 acres in the center of the development as open space. Plan Three, which the firm favors, Caton said, is called the hamlet subdivision. This plan proposes sixty-two mixed-use building units on approximately 25 acres, leaving the bulk of the property—95 acres—as farmland. The innovative plan includes a building designed as and resembling a typical barn in the region that could be divided into apartments.

Caton's firm also represents two other Hunterdon County communities, the Borough of Readington and Bethlehem Township. Each municipality has an ordinance mandating cluster development in rural or agricultural zones, which means, Caton said, that any subdivision of single-family houses must be limited to 30 percent of the property being developed, leaving 70 percent as farmland or open space.

Neither the hamlet plan for Delaware Township nor the cluster developments in the other communities create a true neighborhood development, since none of the plans calls for neighborhood commercial development and community facilities, and the two cluster ordinances do not call for a mix of housing units. However, all three approaches are ways to permit development while preserving valuable farmland and open space. A hamlet-type development may be an especially wise choice for those municipalities where development takes place farm by farm, said Caton, as opposed to a municipality considering a TDR plan that dictates development in all or most of the municipality.

Anton C. Nelessen's business card lists the initials already mentioned, plus a master's degree in architecture from Harvard; it advertises "visioning, planning and urban design." His firm, A. Nelessen Associates, is located on the top floor (the first floor is his home) of a long, white building located in Belle Mead, Somerset County, alongside a creek where, on an early spring day, shad swim upstream. Instead of talking about smart growth, everyone's term for controlled and sensible development, Nelessen speaks of a smart code that regards land as if it were composed of different slices, each slice representing a unique quality and best possible use. For example, one slice, which he calls land-preserve, includes environmentally sensitive wetlands, endangered species of wildlife, and what he refers to as "legacy woods." This slice, he said, must be preserved forever in its natural state. A second slice includes farmland. "This is open space," Nelessen said, "land we don't need for growth, at least not for the foreseeable future." It's land held in trust, not only for its value as farmland, but also because people need to see it and feel it for its "unfettered beauty. It's better than a van Gogh painting," he said.

This second slice, preserved farmland and open space, could be the sending district for a TDR plan such as that in Chesterfield Township and elsewhere, the source of development rights to be used by the so-called New Urbanists to develop a traditional neighborhood center. The smart code also might rid the land of such haphazard and potentially disastrous (from the standpoint of intelligent planning) zoning nomenclature as R-1 and R-2, Nelessen said. For example, a farmer owning a large tract of land should be able to set aside a portion of his spread for a small cluster of houses to be built in close proximity to his farmstead and existing outbuildings, which already constitute a cluster. "If we do [the visioning, planning and design] right, we won't have to touch another acre of farmland for two hundred years," said Nelessen.

The Garden State and its farming legacy may have to bank on Nelessen and other planners doing it right. Nelessen began doing his part some twenty-five years ago in Washington Township, Mercer County, when he first conceived of a town center bordering that portion of Route 33 between Route 130 in the east and the border with Hamilton Township in the west, but his vision remained mostly just that, a vision. Now, in the capable hands of other planners and designers, the town center is nearing completion and, in 2005, became the receiving district for a TDR program intended to save remaining farmland (sending district) that totals several thousands of acres and is planted mostly in soybeans, feed corn, and sod for landscaping. The township, like Chesterfield Township in Burlington County, is a crucible where TDR and TND will be tested and perhaps become another working model for that combination throughout the state.

Robert Melvin of Melvin/Kernan Development Strategies in Thorofare, Gloucester County, took over where Nelessen left off and is primarily responsible for the design that now guides the development of Washington's town center. "Around the mid-eighties, Washington Township was thrown a huge project," said Melvin, "and they saw it as a threat; their rural heritage was going to be consumed by suburban sprawl." The huge project was a sixteen hundred-planned-unit development. "For a while, they were scrambling around trying to figure out how to effectuate appropriate development [that could also save the township's remaining farmland], and their first response was to try and do it through litigation, by suing developers. They lost just about every court case and found out that you don't effectuate good community design or balance of community [with farmland and open space] through adversarial fighting, but rather through proactive planning. That's when I arrived on the scene."

�֎ *Washington Township Builds Its Town Center*

In the summer of 2005, the statue of a World War I doughboy stood at attention on the point formed by the juncture of County Road 526 and State Highway 33 in Washington Township. He stared west, and what his cold, bronze eyes saw then was State Highway 33, but about to become the main street of Washington's town center. The traditional neighborhood that flanks what used to be Highway 33 (which was to be rerouted as a bypass) is not quite what the doughboy would have grown up in, but has some similar characteristics. The housing units consist of a side-by-side mix of detached single-family dwellings, townhouses, and duplexes, and the residents of those units can walk—not drive—to retail stores along main street and to the twenty-two parks and gardens. You can see picket fences and front porches but no garages. Cars park on the street or in garages out of sight.

The whole point of the town center and the TDR program that feeds it, said John West, township administrator, is to save farmland in this twenty-two-square-mile municipality that is bordered by Interstate 195 and the New Jersey Turnpike and has become a desirable hometown for people commuting north to Newark and New York City and west to Trenton and Philadelphia. In his office in the spring of 2005, West pointed to a sizable piece of land adjacent to the main street of the town center colored white on a planning (as opposed to zoning) map tacked to the wall in his office. "A developer recently purchased about 450 acres of farmland, and out of those acres he has agreed to preserve as farmland about 370 acres."

"The town center is the engine for protecting farmland and open space," said Melvin. "During my tenure [he is now working to save farmland in Woolwich Township, Gloucester County] we saved three thousand to five thousand acres of farmland and open space, some preserved under Green Acres. TDR will save even more." Sharbell Development Corporation, which has been the major developer in the town center, was scheduled to purchase ninety development rights from the township's TDR bank before the end of 2005 to complete its plan for more than eight hundred units in the town center. According to Tom Troy, senior vice president of Sharbell, the ninety development rights, or easements, represent three hundred acres of preserved farmland.

✻ TDR Planned for Other Municipalities

Washington Township is one of five municipalities declared a TDR demonstration site by the state Department of Community Affairs in 2005. Only three are designed primarily to save farmland; the others, besides Washington Township, are Woolwich Township in Gloucester County and Hopewell Township in Cumberland County. What the designation means is that the state will pay for the kind of professional planning that the likes of Anton Nelessen and Robert Melvin can provide. Ted Ritter, Hopewell Township administrator, is the first to admit that his township probably couldn't afford a professional planner out of its own budget.

Woolwich Township's twenty-one square miles are situated at the western end of Gloucester County, and most of those square miles are squeezed in between the New Jersey Turnpike and Interstate 295. Native Americans lived along the banks of the Raccoon Creek until they were displaced by Swedes, who came in sufficient numbers during the seventeenth century to populate a village they called, naturally, Swedesboro (exit 2 off the turnpike). Today, Swedesboro is a separate, incorporated municipality that is surrounded by Woolwich Township. The town, for which the historic King's Highway serves as its main street, has managed to survive and actually flourish even though the agricultural industry in the surrounding township, which once supplied a Del Monte processing plant, has significantly declined in the last twenty years. Jane Di Bella, township clerk, whose husband farms 250 acres consisting primarily of tomatoes and peppers on Russell Mill Road, remembers a time when trucks laden with tomatoes would stand in line at the Swedesboro Auction for most of the day. "Now, you might see three or four trucks; it takes about ten minutes. It's kind of sad." Her husband trucks his produce to the Vineland Auction in Cumberland County, about twenty-five miles south.

Despite Del Monte's exit from the area and the departure of the food processing industry generally from South Jersey, Woolwich still thinks of itself as primarily a farming community. Of the township's 13,731 acres, nearly 52 percent were actively devoted to agriculture in 2002. That figure was down only slightly at the end of 2005. The Woolwich Web site boasts that the township has "some of the most fertile soil in the state." It goes on to virtually promise that township officials will protect this "finite and irreplaceable natural resource which is important, not only to the growing of many different kinds of fruits and produce, but also for the economy of the farmers who enjoy tilling the soil."

In 2003, Woolwich Township officials decided to take a fresh look at the township's master plan. They came away shaking their heads after discovering that, without drastic revision, the plan would allow the population to balloon to 70,000, double the number that township officials then envisioned or wanted and a number that almost certainly would wipe out nearly all of the township's prime farmland. As it is, the township leads the state—and now the entire East Coast—in spectacular growth. It is estimated by the township that the population more than doubled in five years, from approximately three thousand in the year 2000 to over six thousand in the year 2005. The main reason for the spurt, and why the population is still expanding rapidly, is Weatherby, a planned 4,500-unit development along Center Square Road, now a thoroughfare that was once a country road beginning in the west at a dot on the map called Center Square Station and ending in the east at King's Highway. In 2005, Weatherby was not quite half completed.

Woolwich mayor Joseph Chila, who moved to the township before Weatherby and other developments began gobbling up farmland, was quoted by a newspaper reporter in 2004 as saying, "Most of our township is still rural, and we desperately need to save it. I can still look out my window and see a wheat field. I may not be able to do that forever, but I'll enjoy it while I can." Robert Melvin, the same planner who designed Washington Township's town center, was hired by Woolwich Township to help ensure that Chila's view remains a wheat field for many years beyond the mayor's tenure.

In the spring of 2005, Melvin, who thinks of himself as a "community builder" and is paid from the state's TDR demonstration grant, began with the township's 2003 master plan as his guide. The plan refers to two town centers, similar to but not necessarily patterned after Washington Township's town center. One is expected to consist primarily, if not exclusively, of the extensive Weatherby development; presumably, Center Square Road would become that town center's main street. Center Square Road already is a main street of sorts for Beckett New Towne, the major development just west of Weatherby in Logan Township. Indeed, according to Woolwich Township's Web site, Woolwich's 1973 master plan projected the township's becoming a "bedroom community" serving neighboring Logan Township's commercial development, particularly the Pureland Industrial Complex, which converted fifty-five farms into 150 commercial tenants in one hundred buildings on three thousand acres.

🐾 *New Town Center Envisioned*

In late fall of 2005, Melvin presented to the Township Committee a plan for a second town center along old U.S. Route 322, starting at exit 2 of the New Jersey Turnpike and extending west for several miles. The design calls for an eventual town center population of five thousand to eight thousand persons, all housed in condominiums and townhouses or in apartments located over stores and offices. The center would not include any single-family, detached homes. Approximately one thousand units would be restricted to persons over age fifty-five.

At a town meeting in June 2005, township residents voiced concern about any new development that would substantially increase the number of children in the township and, consequently, require the construction of yet another elementary school. The median age of Woolwich Township residents is thirty-three, and the median family income is $87,000, according to Mayor Chila. The huge Weatherby community still under construction and other, smaller developments have produced schoolfuls of children and caused the township to greatly expand all municipal services, but few new businesses have opened. In response to township newcomers in the audience that night who have seen their local taxes increase sharply, Mayor Chila complained that the developers of Weatherby still haven't counted "enough rooftops" (a means for predicting commercial viability) to justify the building of more business enterprises. As of late fall 2005 the CVS Pharmacy at the corner of Center Square Road and Auburn Road was the only visible sign of commerce generated by Weatherby. However, a number of new businesses opened in neighboring Logan Township during 2005.

According to Melvin, the town center along Route 322 would require one thousand to thirteen hundred credits from developers who want to build there. The developers must purchase the credits from township farmers who agree to preserve their land. "We estimate the project will ultimately save between three thousand and four thousand acres of farmland," he said.

Melvin's plan addresses two major concerns raised at the June town meeting: what to do about traffic on Route 322 and the need for a sewerage system capable of serving such a large population. Route 322 is a two-lane highway that is a major artery between eastern Pennsylvania and Jersey shore towns. As such, traffic is especially heavy during summer months. Eventually, Melvin said, Route 322 might become a four-lane highway where it borders the town center, but in any event his plan calls for interior roads paralleling Route 322 that will keep most of the town center traffic off the highway.

The state's Smart Growth Plan designates much of the land along the Route 322 corridor as being either in a Fringe Planning Area or a Rural Planning Area. Both areas prohibit installation of sewerage systems. According to Melvin, that prohibition may be waived if township officials, with the weighty help of state legislators representing Gloucester County, can convince state planners and the Department of Environmental Protection that a new sewerage system, or an expansion of the system that now serves the borough of Swedesboro, not only will not harm the surrounding area but actually may be beneficial to neighboring farmland. In these times, when science and local governments both have come to realize that water is a resource requiring greater protection from overuse and abuse, Melvin's plan suggests that treated water from the town center's sewerage system could irrigate land as opposed to being piped into a waterway that would take it away into the Delaware River.

While much of the commercial property would be contained in the town center along Route 322, some of it would also radiate south from the highway along roads, such as King's Highway, that pass through Swedesboro. The objective, said Melvin, is to allow residents of Swedesboro to also benefit from those stores and offices that would be attracted to the development.

✻ *Preserving Farmland in Cumberland County*

In Cumberland County, which ranks first among the twenty-one counties in number of nurseries and nursery stock acreage and second in several categories of Jersey Fresh, Hopewell Township has the same deadline as Woolwich Township and the other municipalities that received TDR planning grants. It is the most rural of all, and one of the very few municipalities in the state that has actually zoned farmland for agriculture instead of houses. Ted Ritter, township administrator and kin to the Ritter family that once owned and operated the Ritter cannery in neighboring Bridgeton, believes TDR is the answer for Hopewell farmers, most of whom, he said, "want to farm."

TDR should be more successful in his area than the state's traditional and still primary strategies for farmland preservation, Ritter said. Local farmers have complained in the past that, even though they live and work in the number one farming county, the state offers them considerably less an acre for a standard preservation easement than it pays farmers in northern counties. Ritter echoed the criticism heard often among South Jersey farmers that the state is positively niggardly when it comes to assessing farmland below Interstate 195, the arbitrary line that separates the state into north and south as it travels east from Trenton at sixty-five miles an hour to the coast. Of course, South Jersey farmers forget or overlook the fact that not only land but nearly everything else is much more expensive north of that arbitrary dividing line.

Clarke•Caton•Hintz is the firm hired by Hopewell Township to devise its TDR plan. Hopewell, like most other rural communities in Cumberland and Salem counties, has in the past not been bothered much by developers anxious to build houses on the counties' prime farmland (together, Cumberland and Salem counties rank first among all twenty-one counties in the production of thirteen out of twenty-two crops). However, as the counties to the north, particularly Gloucester County, fill up with housing, developers have turned to the fertile south. Philip Caton is convinced that TDR came to Hopewell, and perhaps soon to all of Cumberland and Salem counties, "just in time." Caton's firm and the municipality are committed to preserving all land in the agriculture zone that has not yet been preserved through a combination of state, county, and municipal easement purchases (the township and its taxpayers already have committed tens of thousands of dollars to farmland preservation).

The receiving district for Hopewell Township's TDR program will consist mostly of land that is contiguous to the township's border with the city of Bridgeton, the county seat. Unlike Woolwich Township, Hopewell's planned receiving district is not only eligible for water and sewerage systems from Bridgeton, but the city already services existing homes along its border and businesses along State Route 49, which runs through Hopewell Township and Bridgeton and connects the New Jersey Turnpike and Delaware Memorial Bridge in the west with the shore in the east.

Caton estimates that one credit will be awarded for every six acres of farmland that a landowner in the agricultural zone—the sending district—agrees to preserve through the TDR program, a ratio similar to that established in Chesterfield, the TDR pioneer. Of course, no one can predict what each credit might be worth, but the last credits sold by landowners in Chesterfield were in excess of $50,000. Owners of farmland in the sending district who demonstrate that they are under especially heavy pressure from developers to sell their land outright may be entitled to a "bonus" if they agree to sell credits, or development rights, instead of their farm, said Caton.

"Development is knocking at our door," said Ted Ritter, township administrator, "and the way we look at it is that every house that's not built on farmland maintains a tradition and quality of life for Hopewell Township." He and the municipal governing body and planning board hope farmers and developers alike will buy into the TDR program. "Whether we can get everybody in the boat rowing with oars at the same time, who the hell knows. We sure hope it works."

Whether TDR and/or TND will become acceptable plans in other municipalities in Cumberland and Salem counties, which are working very hard to keep their best farmland out of the hands of developers using the state's traditional preservation program, the hard fact is that many officials and longtime residents in those counties are fearful that whatever they do may not be "just in time." In June 2004, the Salem County Agriculture Development Board and the nonprofit citizens group Preservation Salem sponsored a widely publicized "dialog" to consider how—or whether—the county's "quality of life" could be preserved while balancing smart growth and farmland preservation. In a full-page announcement about the program in the local newspaper, the organizations laid out choices and possible consequences:

> If all land in the county were converted to housing tracts, it would be difficult for residents to find jobs nearby, it would be very inconvenient to shop, and food would be more expensive because of the lack of local agriculture. . . . Traffic congestion would be crippling, residents would be adversely affected by a lack of open areas [in which] to exercise and enjoy recreational activities, and the air, land and water may become polluted. However, if all the land were preserved for farms, the population would remain very low, job choice would be limited to agriculture occupations only, and there would be few cultural, education[al] or vocational opportunities nearby.

The statement called for a necessary balance and a close working relationship between state, county, and municipalities, "so that all programs, ordinances, and plans fit together like a well-crafted puzzle."[5]

✳ *Updating the State Plan*

However, those working on a jigsaw puzzle usually know what the completed puzzle is supposed to look like when all the pieces are fitted together because the cover of the box from which the pieces came displays the completed picture. Unfortunately, no one knows for certain what the "well-crafted puzzle" that the Salem County organizations were hoping for is supposed to look like. The state's Development and Redevelopment Plan, first adopted in 1992, was intended to help shape the future direction of development and to help ensure a balance between such development and land preservation. What came to be called simply the State Plan was to be updated every three years by state agencies, counties, and municipalities working together to reexamine and possibly to revise local master plans, zoning ordinances, and other planning documents so that they reflected the purposes of the State Plan. It took nine years for the first update to be completed, in 2001, and the second revision was not scheduled to be completed until 2006. In a way, said Paul Drake, planning director for the Office of State Planning, the process becomes a "never fulfilling prophecy," like a jigsaw puzzle where those piecing it together are never quite sure what exactly the completed puzzle is supposed to look like, or whether, in fact, it will ever be completed.

In November 2003, Dominick J. Sassi, a resident of Carneys Point in Salem County and presently a member of the township's Planning Board, wrote a very long letter to the editor of the county newspaper in which he commented upon the so-called ratables chase, which he predicted would end only in higher property taxes for everyone, and the great disparity between what the county and state will pay the farmer to preserve his land and what a developer will pay the same farmer to build houses on it. He concluded by urging county residents to become educated about smart growth and to join with all those attempting to find and maintain that balance between development and agriculture. "Time is not on your side," he warned.[6]

A year and eight months after that letter appeared, Albert Costill, a farmer in Pilesgrove Township, Salem County, wrote a letter to the editor to say that time had run out on him and his family farm. He complained that he and other farmers were getting shortchanged by supermarket chains that buy cheap from farmers and sell dear to consumers, and he echoed Sassi's lament that state and county preservation agencies combined cannot come close to matching the money the farmer can earn by selling his land to a developer. "Several years ago, we [he and his family] attempted to put our farm into Farmland Preservation, but we were told that it was not enough acres to [qualify for the program]. This is the same field [on which] developers are going to put twenty-one houses on two-acre lots." Costill predicted that more and more of New Jersey's and America's farms will fall victim to "houses and malls." He ended with this plea: "Something must be done."[7]

"Always a Call to the Land" ❧ CHAPTER 6

W hen European settlers first arrived in the "pleasant and profitable country" that became New Jersey and then the Garden State, Leni-Lenape women were planting and harvesting primarily corn, beans, and squash, what Native Americans referred to as the "three sisters." Five centuries later, one cannot be certain what are the three sisters in the Garden State, except that they are no longer corn, beans, and squash.

One obvious way to identify the three primary crops in the Garden State today is to determine their cash receipts, a statistic that the state Department of Agriculture computes each year. According to the department's 2004 Annual Report, the three crops boasting the highest cash receipts in 2003 were blueberries ($46 million), tomatoes ($28 million), and bell peppers ($26 million). Incidentally, the cash receipts for field corn totaled $7 million, but that crop might come close to regaining the position it enjoyed five hundred years ago if ethanol becomes a substitute for or additive to gasoline on a grand scale in the near future, as some predict and strive for (see Chapter Seven). Still another way one might possibly calculate the top three crops is to compare New Jersey production with that of the other forty-nine states. Using that standard, the Garden State ranks second among all the states in blueberry production and third in cranberries and bell peppers; New Jersey stands fourth in production of head lettuce and fifth in freestone peaches. On the other hand, cash receipts from greenhouses, nurseries, and Christmas tree farms account for more than a third of the total agricultural cash receipts in the Garden State for 2003 ($368 million out of $846 million). But then, one must consider the fact that New Jersey is the nation's major supplier of quality turf-grass source material, and the many-faceted turf-grass industry—or green industry—not only constitutes a sizable chunk of the agricultural economy, but is a major factor in the overall state economy. Finally, we can't overlook the fact that New Jersey is a worldwide producer of top-grade asparagus seed.

By any measure, however, agriculture in this first decade of the twenty-first century remains a major and flourishing industry in this most urban state, in large part because enough people are doing just enough to help maintain the delicate balance between development and agriculture. The total cash receipts of $846 million in 2003 were down 3 percent from 2002 but more than $100 million over 1999. In any given year, crop yields and cash receipts may vary widely according to weather conditions, prevalence of disease and insects, costs of doing business, and, of course, market demand. With a shrug and a raise of his eyebrows, Dennis Doyle, manager of the Atlantic Blueberry Company, spoke for every farmer in New Jersey and elsewhere who is at the mercy of elements beyond their control: "Agriculture is, after all, agriculture."

To begin our focus on the state of the gardens in the Garden State, I have arbitrarily created for consideration here a composite, contemporary three sisters consisting of selections from the examples cited above. Two entries on my list are among New Jersey's oldest yet consistently most popular crops, blueberries and cranberries; my third choice, the turf-grass industry, also has roots—literally—going back decades if not centuries, but the widespread popularity of these grasses across the country is of more recent vintage, identified now with seed and sod for home lawns, golf courses, parks, sports stadiums, and anywhere else where turf grass flourishes. Not at all coincidentally, all three crops have relied heavily for their continued success and prominence in the marketplace on the research conducted by Cook College of Rutgers–the State University, and Rutgers's Agricultural Experiment Station, which, for 125 years, has helped farmers exercise whatever control over the elements they are able to effect and also has enabled them to be more productive, regardless of what crop they sow or reap. Recall what Professor Schermerhorn did for the tomato.

✳ Taming the Blueberry

Many of the same Leni-Lenape women who harvested corn, beans, and squash in the fall had, earlier in the summer, picked wild blueberries, which they found growing on waist-high bushes in the sand down among the pine and cedar trees not far from the ocean. The Native Americans, of course, didn't know or particularly care why these tasty berries, whose juice also made a passable paint or ink, grew so well in that particular environment and not so well farther inland. Indeed, it wasn't until early in the twentieth century that anyone figured out with any degree of certainty why the blueberry bushes of the New Jersey pinelands were more plentiful and bountiful there than in almost any other place.

"The Wild Blueberry Tamed" is the title of an article that appeared in the June 1916 issue of *The National Geographic Magazine.* The subtitle reads, "The New Industry of the Pine Barrens of New Jersey." The author of the article, Frederick V. Coville, a botanist with the U.S. Department of Agriculture, stated that five years earlier he had written his first article about the blueberry bush, in which he admitted that no one could figure out why, "when given the kind of care, protection, and nourishment usually bestowed on cultivated crops, the blueberry sickens and dies." Finally, it was learned, he stated, that "the healthy blueberry plant has on its roots a minute fungus, invisible without the aid of a compound microscope, which, unlike most fungi, appears to be beneficial . . . its particular beneficent action being to furnish nitrogenous food to the blueberry bush." The next step, wrote Coville, was to determine what soil was most accommodating to the fungus. "The blueberry fungus requires an acid soil, and it thrives best in one composed of leaf peat and sand. The pine barrens of New Jersey afford just that kind of soil."[1]

Coville and his associates at the U.S. Department of Agriculture knew that the pine barrens (now referred to as the pinelands) had the right soil for blueberry bushes worthy of cultivation because of the contributions made by Elizabeth C. White, a resident of New Lisbon in Burlington County. White, in 1910, saw a USDA bulletin that reported on the blueberry fungus experimentation over the past four years. The bulletin may have been sent to her father, who was a cranberry grower. According to a USDA bulletin in 1921, in which Coville traced the history of early experimentation, "Miss White at once perceived the significance of the experiments and the importance of testing their application to the waste lands surrounding her father's cranberry bogs." The USDA reached an agreement with White in 1913, and field testing began with twenty thousand different hybrid seedlings planted on sixteen acres owned by White's father in Whitesbog, four miles south of Browns Mills in Burlington County. "Thus far," wrote Coville, "about eighteen thousand of these hybrids have fruited, and four of them have been selected and approved as worthy of introduction into agriculture."[2]

Until the connection could be made between the fungus and the soil, Coville wrote in *The National Geographic Magazine*, it wasn't possible to establish an "industry of blueberry culture." In other words, up until the successful field testing in Whitesbog on the White property, blueberry picking had remained pretty much as primitive as it was in the days of the Leni-Lenape. No farmer was making any money growing blueberry bushes. One other problem remained, however, according to Coville. If a farmer was to "set out a whole field with plants from cuttings of a single choice bush, his plantation would be practically fruitless, because it would contain no other blueberry stock from which the bees in their search for nectar could bring the unrelated pollen required to enable his choice plants to set fruit. The best procedure is to make up the plantation with alternating rows of plants propagated by cuttings from two choice varieties. Each will then set fruit in abundance through pollination by the other."[3]

Now that modern science circa 1916, along with the considerable assistance of Elizabeth White, had discovered how to grow bushes laden with blueberries on a large scale, Coville was able to promise his readers and would-be blueberry growers that the blueberry culture "not only promises to add to the general welfare through the utilization of land almost valueless otherwise, but it offers a profitable industry to individual landowners in districts in which general agricultural conditions are especially hard and unpromising."[4]

Today, in Atlantic County, if one drives down back-country roads such as county routes 542 and 559—but even while traveling the Atlantic City Expressway—one will see the fulfillment of Coville's prophecy: thousands of acres of bushes, some shoulder-high, that produce more fresh-market blueberries than any other place in the world (blueberries are also sold frozen). Of course, it took some time for Coville's foresight to be realized. By 1927, eleven years after his article appeared in *National Geographic Magazine*, Atlantic County growers on the edge of the pinelands were successfully growing several varieties of blueberries, according to Dennis Doyle, who knows his blueberry history. Because the industry in New Jersey and elsewhere—especially in Michigan and North Carolina—was expanding so rapidly, said Doyle, growers formed a cooperative titled Tru-Blu, which "was very large and powerful in the 1940s, fifties, and sixties. The best way to describe it is to say that it was the Ocean Spray of blueberries [Ocean Spray is a cranberry cooperative]."

The Atlantic Blueberry Company, which Doyle manages, was formed in 1937 by five Galletta brothers, sons of Italian immigrants. They began with five acres. In the summer of 2005, the company—now owned by three descendants of the founders—operated the largest cultivated blueberry farm in the world: fourteen hundred acres of high bushes. (In Maine and Nova Scotia, farmers grow a smaller blueberry on low bushes.) Blueberries are picked from mid to late June through early September, the harvest period depending on weather.

Atlantic Blueberry Company and other growers are expanding the market for high-bush blueberries with the assistance of the United States High Bush Blueberry Council. Doyle is a past president of the council. "We have cultivated the Japanese market in the last few years, and that's doing very well," said Doyle. "Now we're moving into Taiwan, Korea, and China." The council has some concern about the Chinese market, Doyle said, because of what happened to American apple growers when they courted China. Instead of continuing to import apples from our northwestern states, Doyle said, the Chinese decided to grow their own apples, which "just about wiped out apple growers in Washington State." To date, the Chinese are interested only in buying blueberries, not growing bushes.

While Tru Blu Cooperative Association in its heyday and the United States High Bush Blueberry Council today are largely responsible for the development and expansion of the market for fresh and frozen blueberries, the Philip E. Marucci Center for Blueberry and Cranberry Research and Extension is primarily responsible for maintaining the health of the blueberry. The center, located deep inside the pinelands, is one of nine divisions of the Agricultural Experiment Station (AES). Dr. Nicholi Vorsa was its director in 2005.

In the early 1930s, not long after high-bush blueberry cultivation began to blossom as an industry, it was in danger of being obliterated by blueberry stunt disease. A history of the AES reported:

> At first the symptoms were not alarming, for though plants looked sickly, they continued to live and produce in a limited way. It was thought at first that they simply needed more nourishment, but in 1942 a [U.S. Department of Agriculture] scientist, Raymond B. Wilcox, diagnosed the trouble as a virus disease, and the hunt was on to find the insect that carried it. In 1947, the New Jersey Blueberry Cooperative Association appropriated five thousand dollars annually for a three-year study, and [Philip E.] Marucci [of the AES] was engaged specifically to concentrate on the problem.[5]

Through relentless research, Marucci concluded that the disease was carried by an insect called the leafhopper. The only problem was that Marucci also identified sixty varieties of leafhopper. Which one was the carrier? Or which ones? "For six long discouraging years the disease spread relentlessly, and the hunt went on without the discovery of any positive evidence as to which of the sixty species of hoppers was the [culprit]," stated the report. "Then, in the sixth year, the field was narrowed to two species, and Martin T. Hutchinson [also of the AES] determined one of the two to be the culprit. Once identified, it was not too difficult to figure out the right spray to destroy the hoppers."[6]

Today, the Marucci Center is still focused on ways to identify and combat diseases that might threaten the blueberry and cranberry industries, including that old nemesis, the leafhopper, which also can infect and stunt the growth of the cranberry plant. In the last twenty or so years, Vorsi said, blueberry growers, and therefore the center, also have been concerned about something called the scorch virus. "It's a major viral problem here in New Jersey," he said, "and in the Pacific Northwest as well." The carrier in this case is an aphid. "When I was here in the 1980s as a graduate student and assistant professor, there was a large population of aphids in the fields. At the time, we thought they were simply a nuisance; we had no idea they were [spreading] a viral disease." Farmers were spraying their fields from the air, and coverage on the plants was not the best, said Vorsi, so most of the aphids survived. In the summer of 2005, Vorsi and others on his staff were observing blueberry plants collected elsewhere along the Atlantic seaboard that appeared to be resistant to the aphid carrying the virus. Once again, the AES scientists went to work to find a better way to rid blueberry bushes of the aphid.

✱ Giving Thanks for Cranberries

Centuries before Americans sat down to a Thanksgiving Day turkey dinner with all the trimmings, which usually included cranberries in some form, the great king, or sachem, of the Leni-Lenape Nation in New Jersey served cranberries to dinner guests from the Iroquois Nation to the north and the Cherokee Nation to the south. The king's major task in life was to keep the peace between the Leni-Lenape and the other nations. "This [keeping of the peace] necessitated frequent state feasts at which cranberries were always eaten. In time, cranberries began to be associated with these feasts of peace." And they were definitely associated with the king, because his name, Pakimintzen, translates as Cranberry Eater.[7]

Early settlers from Europe were quick to discover the cranberry, which grew profusely on the shores of Barnegat Bay and in the swamps and along the riverbanks in what was then called the pine barrens; indeed, they relished them so much that they often began picking them before they were ripe. This practice prompted the state legislature to pass a law in 1789 that "forbade the picking of cranberries before 10 October, [violators] of which would incur a ten shilling fine."[8] Ordinarily, cranberry harvest in New Jersey still does not begin until early October.

The first attempts to cultivate the cranberry occurred in the 1830s. One of the industry pioneers was John J. Webb, known as Peg Leg John because of his one wooden leg. According to historian Paul Eck, "the story has it that Peg Leg John had difficulty in moving his cranberries from his storage loft to the packing area located below because of his handicap. He resorted to bouncing the berries down the stairs rather than carrying them down. The sound berries bounced to the bottom of the stairs, whereas the rotted fruit became hung up on the treads. D. T. Stanford used this bounce principle to develop the first cranberry separator. The principle is still in use today to separate soft cranberries from sound fruit."[9]

It wasn't until the 1860s, however, with the onset of the American Civil War, that the cranberry industry in New Jersey began to expand rapidly in and around little pinelands crossroads with picturesque names like Ongs Hat and Hog Wallow. In 1875, New Jersey growers produced 36,667 barrels of cranberries, compared to 25,000 in New England and 15,000 in the western states. Of course, cranberry yield, like that for any other agricultural product, can vary considerably from year to year. Three years later, in 1878, New Jersey production was down to 20,000 barrels and New England's yield had increased to 41,666 and the western states' to 36,923. In 2003, the New Jersey cranberry industry ranked third among all states in total value of production, at $15.1 million, behind Wisconsin and Massachusetts.

While cranberry vines in New Jersey are found almost exclusively in the pinelands of Burlington County, an anomaly was reported by the *Daily Times* of New Brunswick in May 1880. The newspaper quoted Circular #1 from the Agricultural Experiment Station, which stated that, at a recent meeting of the station's directors, mention was made that "on a recent visit to the farm of the late Chalkley Albertson near Haddonfield [the visitor's] attention was called to a deposit of 'poison marl.' This marl destroyed all vegetation when applied in the ordinary way as a top dressing for crops. [The visitor] was also informed that piles of the marl, which have been lying out and exposed to the weather for some years were now covered with a luxuriant growth of cranberries." The report further stated that analysis of the piles of marl indicated a very low pH factor. Indeed, the pH factor, which measures the level of acidity or alkalinity in the soil, rarely goes above a reading of five in soil where cranberries thrive. On the other hand, most vegetables require soil with a pH reading of at least seven.

As is the case with most crops in the twenty-first century, cranberries are now harvested primarily by machine. In the early days, they were harvested in dry bogs by workers wielding hand-held scoops. According to Raymond J. Samulis, agricultural agent for Burlington County, hand harvesting with wooden scoops was "backbreaking work," and the scoops "damaged vines from the pulling action, and many berries were dropped." Currently, the berries are harvested by a machine with a reel head that is twenty feet across and operates in bogs that have been flooded so that the berries rise to the top and float on the surface.[10]

The same blunt-nose leafhopper that can plague blueberries can also spread a disease called false blossom to cranberries. The damage occurs when flower parts are malformed, thus preventing development of sound fruit. While false blossom has been controlled primarily through insecticides, the Marucci experiment station in the pinelands is currently working on a means of eradicating another nemesis: fruit worm larvae that eat both leaves and fruit. Scientists thus far have identified a chemical released by a female moth that attracts the male; their mating produces the larvae that then attack the cranberries. In their testing to date, the scientists have attempted to confuse male moths by inundating an area with the female chemical. According to Dr. Vorsi of the station, "essentially, what happens is that the male cannot find a female; so, if the male cannot find a female, there's no mating, and if there's no mating, there are no eggs and no larvae."

Cranberry growers in New Jersey organized the American Cranberry Growers' Association in 1871. At the time, cranberries were often sold fresh, and at a January 1902 meeting of the association in

Philadelphia, the association's president, the Reverend E. H. Durell, waxed poetic in describing the fruit: "The taste of the cranberry is so delicate, gratifying, charming and exhilarating that among fruits it has no peer. The strongest words may be used and used in the superlative degree, and yet come far short of the reality."[11] Most growers here and around the country are represented today by Ocean Spray Cranberries, Inc., which has its headquarters in Lakeville, Massachusetts, and much of what growers harvest is marketed under the Ocean Spray label as cranberry sauce and juice. In 2005, the cooperative was searching for partners that could help it develop new products and assist in marketing and distribution.

🍂 *Where Turf Grasses Go to Breed*

In 1934, the newly elected mayor of New York City, Fiorello LaGuardia, put Robert Moses in charge of the city's rundown parks, including and especially Central Park, which at the time, according to the Central Park Web site, was "a near ruin, whose lawns, unseeded, were expanses of bare earth, decorated with scraggly patches of grass and weeds, that became dust bowls in dry weather and mud holes in wet." One of the first actions taken by Moses was to reseed the lawns. More than thirty years later, a young C. Reed Funk, who, in 1961, had become the first designated plant breeder at Rutgers University's Cook College ("I was as good a candidate as anybody, I guess") talked the grounds crew at Central Park into allowing him to walk over the park's lawns looking for particularly healthy examples of ryegrass growing low to the ground. Funk, now in his seventies, believes the samples he collected to bring back to Rutgers probably dated from around the 1930s, perhaps when the reseeding took place. However, William A. Meyer, who succeeded Funk as director of the Rutgers Plant Science Research and Extension Farm in Adelphia, Monmouth County, and who now presides over 206 acres of experimental and hybrid turf grasses, thinks the specimens unearthed by his predecessor might have been descendants from European ryegrasses planted in the park a century or two before 1934, which perhaps survived all those years in some ancient "scraggly patches."

In any event, the few plugs of ryegrass from Central Park, which Funk dubbed Manhattan ryegrass, became the nucleus of the ryegrass industry in America, according to Meyer. Before the ground-hugging Manhattan ryegrass perfected by Funk and his associates, all ryegrass in America and Europe had been of the naturally tall variety and was used primarily as forage for grazing cattle. The first pound of Manhattan ryegrass seed was sold in 1967, according to Meyer; "today, it is a 280-million-pound industry, centered mostly in northwestern states, but the breeder seed still comes from this farm." The ryegrass plugs from Central Park were just a few of a number of plugs (germ plasms) of different turf grasses—blue, bent, and fescue—that Funk and others, including Meyer, have brought back to the Experiment Station farm in Adelphia for breeding. Over a forty-year period, Funk has spent perhaps as many as ten thousand hours walking over old turf areas searching for hardy specimens that survived the tests of time, disease, insects, drought, pollutants, and being tread upon. His turf hunting has taken him to cemeteries and village greens, some of which date from colonial times. On one of his expeditions, Funk walked the grounds of the home that once belonged to Henry Wadsworth Longfellow in Cambridge, Massachusetts, and came away with some plugs of fescue. Back at the Adelphia farm, Funk discovered a fungus in the tissue of the fescue grass that not only did not harm the grass but, in fact, enhanced growth and resisted above-ground insects. "The fungus is called an endophyte," said Meyer; "so far, we haven't found an endophyte that will kill grubs below the ground."

Funk, who is revered as a legend by a long list of colleagues past and present, was not the first Rutgers professor to experiment with turf grass. Earlier work had been carried out by G. W. Musgrave, Howard B. Sprague, and Ed Evaul. According to the New Jersey Turfgrass Association, which was officially organized in 1970 and now has six hundred members, out of the work conducted in the Rutgers Agronomy Department and at the Experiment Station in the late 1920s and 1930s, "came studies which demonstrated that turfgrass could be grown on most any soil with proper liming, fertilization, addition of organic matter, and choice of grass."[12] Rutgers initiated a five-day course on turf grass in 1929 that later became a ten-week course. The course was divided into two sections: lawn and utility turf, and golf and fine turf. A two-year course was initiated in 1952, and it continues to be well attended.[13]

The Experiment Station at Adelphia is continually breeding new and better varieties of turf grasses—hundreds so far—and every five years the station enters its best varieties in national trials conducted by the U.S. Department of Agriculture. In recent trials, twenty-nine of the top thirty varieties of fescue and the thirty-five best varieties of ryegrass came from the Adelphia farm. Seed and turf companies are licensed by Rutgers to use the highly prized breeder seed grown at the Experiment Station, and they pay Rutgers royalties for the privilege. In 2004, Meyer said, the university received $2.4 million in royalties, most of which was turned back into research. Daniel Rossi, senior associate director of the Agricultural Experiment Station, estimates that 70 percent of the turf grass and quality grass seed sold in America have their origins in the fields and greenhouses at Adelphia. Meyer believes the figure might be as high as 80 percent. "It's an amazing story," Rossi said.

What is even more amazing are the results of the New Jersey Turfgrass Economic Survey: 2002–2004, conducted by Bruce B. Clarke, specialist in plant pathology at Cook College. He included in the turf-grass industry—what he and others refer to as the green industry—home turf maintenance, home garden plantings and maintenance, golf course maintenance, and sod production. "The Green Industry is a $3.8 billion [a year] industry in New Jersey," he concluded. Here is a summary of Clarke's key findings:

- Total annual revenue for the industry: $1.3 billion.
- Total spent on turf maintenance (homes and golf courses): $1.3 billion.
- Total spent on home plantings and garden maintenance: $1.2 billion.
- Golf courses annually employ more than 14,500 workers, 70 percent of them full time.
- More than 21,000 seasonal workers take care of 349,000 acres of home lawns and earn $400 million in wages, and benefits.

An important component of the turf-grass industry in New Jersey is the forty or so sod growers, whose gross sales from more than 6,500 acres totaled approximately $40 million in 2004, according to Stephen Hart, faculty liaison between the Rutgers Center for Turfgrass Science and the Cultivated Sod Association of New Jersey. The association has been in existence for about thirty years, said Hart, but the sod business can be traced to a time when operators of cemeteries decided that owners of plots would be more pleased if new graves were covered with instant sod rather than having to wait for grass seed to grow—or possibly not. Today, sod growers in New Jersey can be divided into two groups: professional landscapers and those who supply turf for athletic fields.

In 1931, Elmer Betts and his family moved from Connecticut to land along the Tuckahoe River in Atlantic County, and he and his son, Walter, operated a truck farm for the next thirty-five years. By 1967, the family began to switch from vegetables to sod, and within two years, the farm was growing sod only. Today, most of the sod grown by Tuckahoe Turf Farms is on seven hundred acres of sandy loam in blueberry country outside Hammonton. The business is still operated by the Betts family, which employs seventeen full-time and three part-time employees. Automated harvesting machines and pivotal and lateral irrigation machines that roll across fields like giant, skinny dinosaurs save on labor costs and increase profits.

Tuckahoe Turf Farms has supplied sod for a number of sports stadiums, according to James Betts. These include the Phillies and Eagles stadiums in Philadelphia; Fenway Park, home of the Boston Red Sox; Shea Stadium, where the New York Mets play; and football fields owned by the Pittsburgh Steelers, Cleveland Browns, and Green Bay Packers. "We also have provided the sod for a dozen or more minor league fields," Betts said. Most of the stadium sod consists of a blend of four varieties of bluegrass, most if not all of them originating at the Rutgers Agricultural Experiment Station in Adelphia. Bluegrass wears well, said Betts. The family business advertises "fast installation with minimal seams, allowing for the shortest time from installation to usage," and it promises to deliver mature sod in 250-foot-square rolls.

Someone attending the 2005 Rutgers Turfgrass Research Field Day at the Adelphia farm on a hot August day left his peaked cap on a chair. It read: "Rutgers Turfgrass Research: Science•Practice•Success." The motto not only characterizes the relationship between Rutgers and the turfgrass industry, it also serves as a reminder of the long-term connection between Rutgers—specifically Cook College of Agricultural and Environmental Sciences and the Agricultural Experiment Station—and the entire agriculture industry of the Garden State.

The connection was first made after passage of the Morrill Land-Grant Act in 1862. The act, which a farsighted Congress enacted while the nation's immediate focus was on the terrible trials of the American Civil War, granted to each state thirty thousand acres of federal land for each member of Congress from that state. The land was to be sold and the proceeds used to build one or more schools designed to teach "agriculture and the mechanical arts." In the case of New Jersey, the money was used primarily to convert the private Rutgers College, founded in 1766, into a land-grant college. One of the intentions of the Morrill Act, said Daniel Rossi, was to encourage the states to better serve their underserved populations. "At the time," he said, "those persons in agriculture were clearly an underserved population. There was very little science associated with agriculture, so when the land-grant Rutgers University was created, it became primarily a scientific school."

During the Civil War, and for decades after, farming families accounted for well over half the population in New Jersey, Rossi said, probably more like two-thirds. Largely as a result of introducing science to agriculture, he continued, "we found more efficient ways to produce, to increase yields. Clearly, the economic growth of this state and country has come about because of the science and efficiency of our agriculture, for example less labor-intensive agriculture. We released labor that was then able to shift to other parts of the economy, initially into manufacturing, but then eventually into the service industry." The Agricultural Experiment Station, through its research and extension programs, has helped make it possible for the individual farmer and the agriculture industry in general to prosper, Rossi said. "Our job here at the Experiment Station is to continue to try and maintain the Garden State."

As the wording on the peaked cap indicated, the agriculture industry benefits not only from Rutgers research, but also from the applied science offered by the university's faculty, said Chris Carson, Echo Lake Golf Club superintendent and president of the

Tri-State Turf Research Foundation. "This is a partnership that we in the industry appreciate. They [the faculty] hear our problems, understand our problems, and help solve our problems." Carson cited the 1988 case when a previously unknown disease turned New Jersey golf greens brown. "We [golf superintendents] were trying to save our greens and our jobs. We asked Bruce Clarke if he would look at the problem. We were willing to put up the money for research. Rutgers brought in another researcher, who worked with Clarke and others over a two-year period to, first, identify the disease, then develop a means of controlling the disease, and, finally, to identify cultural issues that affected the disease. They identified and solved the problem in an amazing window of time." By defeating the disease through the use of correct chemicals instead of continuing to treat the greens with ineffectual and perhaps even damaging chemicals, the state's golf courses probably saved millions of dollars, said Carson. Also, he said, the Rutgers faculty told course superintendents what fertilizers to use in the future and what general greens care would help prevent the disease from returning. "It's just one example of how science has helped us in the field."

Growing and caring for quality turfgrass is humbling, said Carson, quoting Funk, because "it can change on you in a hurry." Carson is a graduate of Cook College, and he quoted another professor, who reminded his students that when they think they know everything there is to know about turf grass, they should remember that all that anyone really needs in order to grow grass is a crack in the sidewalk.

🐾 New Life for Old Asparagus

New Jersey once ranked number two in the nation in asparagus production, but it is no longer a major fresh-market cash crop for the state's farmers, ranking ninth among eleven fresh-market vegetables in 2004 cash receipts. However, asparagus seed produced by Jersey Asparagus Farms in cooperation with the Rutgers Agricultural Research and Extension Center in Upper Deerfield, Cumberland County, grows quality asparagus throughout the world. Asparagus with names like Jersey Supreme, Jersey Giant, and Jersey Gem is harvested in many countries of Africa, Asia, Europe, and South America, and in several states in this country. Much like the turf-grass seed that has its origins at the Experiment Station in Adelphia, the asparagus seeds come from plants that have been bred and perfected by the Research and Extension Center in Upper Deerfield. The seeds are packaged and shipped by Jersey Asparagus Farms out of a small, nondescript sheet-metal building on the grounds of the old Walker farm, circa 1840, on Porchtown Road in Pittsgrove Township, Salem County.

"Nobody knows what we do here," said Scott Walker, whose family owns Jersey Asparagus Farms. "As far as asparagus goes, worldwide we're known as one of the leaders in asparagus [because of the seed], but around here not too many people know that. They just know us for the [fresh market] spears sold at our roadside stand." Jersey Asparagus Farms sells approximately three thousand pounds of seed annually at $400 per pound. A pound of seed grows an acre of asparagus.

The association between the Walkers and Rutgers began in the early 1970s when the Research and Extension Center was looking for a farm that had never grown asparagus before. For all of its 130 years, the Walker farm had grown just about everything else but. "Rutgers wanted to see how some varieties they had come up with in the laboratory would perform on virgin ground," said Walker. "So they planted them here, and that's how the relationship was struck between us and the original breeder. We continued to work with [Rutgers] and evaluate different varieties [bred at the Research and Extension Center]. In the late 1980s, they asked us if we'd be interested in licensing out the seed—becoming the seed producer. So we did."

Like Reed Funk and William Meyer at Adelphia, who search far and wide for the best plugs of turf grass, Walker tromps over old asparagus fields looking for hardy spears that have survived time, disease, and weather. Some of these fields are in Michigan and Washington State, whose farmers are also purchasers of seed from Jersey Asparagus Farms. "We go into an old, diseased field and look for plants that are still healthy," said Walker. "We look for different things that indicate what the spear quality will be like: the diameter, the color, how much disease is on the plant, which is an indication of disease resistance. When we find good specimens, we dig up the roots and bring them back to the Research and Extension Center. There, they grow the plants and collect pollen off of one plant and put it on another and wait for the seed to develop."

As it has turned out, most of the healthiest roots brought back by Walker were from male plants. "Over time, [Rutgers researchers] found that male plants yield more, live longer, have more disease resistance, and are nicer than female plants. They came up with this certain male that, when crossed with this certain female, would produce all male seeds. So, the seed and crowns that we sell today are male hybrid species. There are a few females mixed in. It's very, very hard to keep something 100 percent male."

❋ *Jersey Fresh, Grown and Organic*

"From the roadside stand to the farmer's market, from the produce aisles of the large grocery store chains to the wooden booth at the county fair, the Garden State's bounty of nutritious, delicious fruits, vegetables and other agricultural products can be found just about anywhere," wrote Agriculture Secretary Charles Kuperus in an editorial carried by newspapers across the state in August 2004. "The reason for this is simple. People know that the one sure way to get the freshest, most delicious products is to buy them close to where they are grown and made. It's what the 'Fresh' in Jersey Fresh is all about." Over the twenty years since the slogan Jersey Fresh was coined, Kuperus stated, "farmers have seen a shift in consumers' attitudes toward products that come from the Garden State." He cited the case of two shoppers in Florida, who go out of their way to buy Jersey Fresh tomatoes or any other vegetable or fruit from New Jersey. "A simple purchase of Jersey tomatoes, peaches, herbs or any of the many other agricultural products from the Garden State supports New Jersey agriculture and [keeps] New Jersey green and growing," he concluded.

Nine months after that editorial appeared, Kuperus announced a new agricultural promotion slogan: Jersey Grown. Speaking at a gathering of nursery and garden center owners in Plainfield in May 2005, Kuperus said, "The Jersey Grown branding program has taken off in popularity, as New Jersey gardeners and residents favor plants, trees and shrubs that are grown by New Jersey farmers."[14] Jersey Grown was designed to promote the ornamental horticultural industry, the largest and fastest growing sector of the agriculture industry in New Jersey. Twenty-three growers were licensed in 2005 to sell their products under the Jersey Grown label. In order to be certified, a grower must demonstrate that his products are grown in New Jersey, have been checked for quality, and are pest and disease free.

For a growing number of consumers, Jersey Fresh doesn't get much fresher or safer and Jersey Grown doesn't grow much better than when products bearing those labels come from the state's fifty-four certified organic farms, whose commodities are sold at nearly seventy community farmers markets. Recent legislation authorized the New Jersey Department of Agriculture to become the official agency to certify organic farms in the state according to standards established by the U.S. Department of Agriculture. For a farm to be certified as organic, the farmer must agree not to use those fertilizers or pesticides that have been found to be detrimental to humans and the environment. The same legislation encouraged the department to create yet another label, Organic Fresh, and to assist farmers who wish to convert from traditional farming to organic farming.

According to the brochure published by the Northeast Organic Farming Association of New Jersey (NOFA-NJ), "We believe farms are ecosystems, not factories. Organic farmers grow crops without synthetic chemicals. Instead, they use methods and materials in harmony with nature." The other methods and materials include alternating crops so as not to wear out the soil (which the Leni-Lenape, of course, practiced centuries ago), "using biological pest and disease controls," and giving organic feed to livestock and poultry. However, "what organic has really been about all along is a mutual contract between farmers and consumers," said Karen Anderson, executive director of NOFA-NJ. The NOFA-NJ office is in Pennington, Mercer County. On Anderson's desk the day of the interview was a copy of the book *Fatal Harvest: the Tragedy of Industrial Agriculture.* Anderson has no argument with the standards set by the federal government and now certified by the state, but she laments that "in the process [of instituting regulations] we lost some of the things that the term organic used to be a shorthand for: local, small scale, generally a family farm; it also meant that social equity and sustainability were core values. Those things didn't make it into the law." The typical organic farm is still smaller than the average farm in New Jersey, just under fifty acres, according to Anderson, compared to the state average of more than eighty acres for all farms.

Although some organic farms, not unlike a number of traditional ones, have gone out of business because of development pressure or because surviving family members had no interest in agriculture, Anderson was obviously pleased to report in the summer of 2005 that three-quarters of the fifty-four certified organic farmers were first generation, who see organic farming has fulfilling some personal goals. "I think there is always a call to the land—to agriculture. Sometimes it might be a romantic notion of what farming is, but there is something so grounded, so literal, and so productive about farming." Before joining NOFA-NJ, Anderson was what she called an information worker. "Being an information worker may be very twentieth century, but it's also very ungrounded; it's somewhere out there in the ether. I think many of us feel a longing to work in something literal, to work out of doors, to commune with nature." She got out of the information business and worked on a farm for two years. "I was a single mom at the time and had an eight-year-old. I didn't have enough capital to purchase a piece of land, and most of the farms around here don't provide housing. The prospect of commuting to a farm while juggling child-care responsibilities was, I decided, not going to work." The alternative was the position with NOFA-NJ. However, Anderson has no lasting regrets. "I think I'm a policy wonk at heart anyway."

One first-generation organic farmer, Jim Kinsel, now manages what is believed to be the largest Community Supported Agricultural (CSA) program in the nation (twenty-two hundred shares representing nearly four thousand individuals in 2005) based at the sixty-acre organic Honey Brook Farm in Pennington. Kinsel heard the "call to the land" in 1990 while capitalizing on his degree in math and computer science by working for Prudential Life Insurance in Newark. "I was in the actuarial department for a couple of years until I got so bored I just wanted to get the hell out of there. So, I worked on a farm for the summer and decided that was what I wanted to do. I worked with area growers, kind of learning, and then the opportunity came along to come to what was then called the Watershed Organic Farm in Pennington." At the time Kinsel arrived at the farm, in 1991, it was the property of the Stony Brook–Millstone Watershed Association.

The customers for Honey Brook Farm produce—sixty crops and more than three hundred varieties of vegetables, fruits and herbs—live as close as Titus Mill Road in Pennington and as far away as eastern Pennsylvania, Montclair in Essex County, and Merchantville in Camden County. Some have purchased individual shares, or memberships, at $322 in 2005; others have bought family or box shares, $518 and $539, respectively. All shares are for a twenty-five week period, and, of course, the individual share of produce is not as large as the family or box shares. Most individual and family shareholders come to the farm and personally select their share of produce from bins that contain fresh vegetables and fruits, or they may sometimes pick strawberries or tomatoes in the field. "We have people driving up in junkers—beat-up cars—and they're pulling in right behind a brand new Porsche," said Kinsel. "This is a kind of locus where these people meet." The shareholders are ethnically and culturally diverse, too. In recent years, Kinsel has witnessed an increase in African Americans, Asians, and newly arrived immigrants from Europe and Central America. The box shares are delivered by Honey Brook Farm to neighborhood locations, where a group of members shares the produce.

Other New Jersey CSAs are Catalpa Ridge Farm in Newfoundland, Passaic County; Emery's Berry Patch (specializing in fresh blueberries and raspberries and everything made from those fruits) in New Egypt, Ocean County; Farmer John's Organic Produce in Warren, Somerset County; Joy's Farm in Paramus, Bergen County; Mill Creek Organic Farm (includes grains and beef) in Medford, Burlington County; and Upper Meadows Farm (includes meat) in Montague, Sussex County.

Twenty-five years ago Bruce Marek considered himself something of an "organic weirdo" when he turned down the chance to apply for a permit to use standard chemicals on the six and a half acres of family-owned land that he intended to farm. "I thought long and hard and decided to respect soil life," he said. While Marek is relatively new at farming, his six and one half acres have been tilled off and on since the Dutch settled the area in the mid-seventeenth century and probably before that when Leni-Lenape women grew their three sisters. Marek's Old Hook Farm is situated on Old Hook Road in Emerson, Bergen County, and his plow still unearths the remains of Dutch clay pipes and pottery. Marek and his wife life in a two-hundred-year-old house near the Pascack Brook, which drains the Pascack Valley in northeastern Bergen County into the Hackensack River.

On his farm, Marek grows collard, kale, and mustard; tomatoes, fifteen varieties of eggplant, including one that originated in Thailand, and other vegetables in season. In addition to those products, Old Hook Farm sells organically grown flowers and shrubs and a variety of natural foods at his roadside market and also at a market in Hoboken, Hudson County. While Old Hook Farm is not an official CSA, Marek believes organic farms like his, because they are so small and specialized, can survive only if they have the loyal support and patronage of consumers who believe in the concept and benefits of organically grown produce. Fortunately for Old Hook Farm, enough of the people who now live in the developments that have nearly eradicated farming in Bergen County are believers.

Some persons may think the term "organic farming" applies only to vegetables and fruits. However, Garden State consumers can also buy poultry, beef, and pork that have been raised according to organic standards. For example, the heritage breed of turkeys and the chickens and beef raised for market by the four hundred-acre Flatbrook Farm in Sussex County are fed "only what nature intended." According to Bob Campbell, who, in 2004, managed the farm owned by Frances and Marvin Naftel and who raised two hundred turkeys, "Turkeys are natural grazers. Grass is the natural food for them. If you watch wild turkeys, you'll notice they'll eat grass, nuts, berries, bugs, and leaves. Having them out on the grass is definitely a great asset for our fields. It aerates and fertilizes the soil, and turkeys don't rip the roots of the grass."[15] Consumers like the Flatbrook turkeys that are as close to being wild as possible, said Campbell. "They're not gamey, and there's a little more fat, a little more flavor. And the meat is a lot denser, not as marbled. Everyone's always real happy with our turkeys."[16]

✿ Jersey Fresh Goes to Market

A goodly portion of Jersey Fresh vegetables, fruits, and herbs grown by farmers in New Jersey's southern counties are sold at auction to brokers representing supermarket chains from Florida to Canada and as far west as Chicago. It all happens six days a week from April to November at the seventy-five-year-old Vineland Produce Auction in Cumberland County, the largest produce auction on the East Coast. The auction is a cooperative owned by approximately two hundred member farmers and managed by Peter Bylone, whose father was on the board of directors from 1954 until he retired in the late 1990s. In an average year, the auction sells seven million packages (crates, boxes, etc.) of produce worth $50 million.

Anyone with vegetables to sell is welcome at the auction, said Bylone. "Everybody is treated equally. If a retired person, or maybe a school teacher who has just a few acres, wants to raise some stuff, they have the ability to come here and sell their produce." All the "stuff" is fresh on the day it is purchased at auction. At the time of the sale, said Bylone, the spinach or tomatoes or squash or whatever may not even have been harvested. If, for example, a farmer gets his price at auction in the morning, he may then have to go back to the farm and load up his truck with whatever the broker purchased. That's Jersey Fresh!

Up until several years ago, the auction was a noisy affair, with brokers shouting out their bids and auctioneers keeping track of the bidding by calling out just as loudly. Today, the auction is computerized—and quiet. Brokers sit in assigned seats in an auditorium—the auction arena—with stadium-like seating. Each broker also has an assigned button that allows him or her to bid on produce described on an easy-to-read screen in the front of the auction arena. Not only has the computer cut down on most of the clamor of the auction, it also has eliminated most of the human error that occurred not infrequently. In the past, Bylone said, brokers sometimes would complain that the auctioneer didn't record their bid, or they might claim that the auctioneer credited them with a bid they didn't make.

✳ A Man of Vision

In 1888, Jacob Goodale Lipman, age fourteen, came to America with his parents to escape the pogroms of czarist Russia and to settle in the six-year-old Alliance Colony in Salem County, across the Maurice River from Vineland. The Lipmans, like the first Jewish families in the colony, had come to farm. Also like the first settlers, they didn't know the first thing about being farmers. Czarist Russia prohibited Jews from owning or cultivating land. In a 1978 magazine article, the late I. Harry Levin, the son of original settlers, wrote, "[The colonists'] idea was to become tillers of the soil and thus shake off the accusation that they were petty mercenaries. . . . Their thought was to live in the open instead of being shut-ins who lived an artificial city life." The Alliance Colony became the first successful Jewish agricultural community in the United States, and Jacob Lipman became the director of the Rutgers Agricultural Experiment Station in 1911 and the first dean of Cook College in 1915. He had graduated from Rutgers University in 1898.

In his first speech to the board of managers of the Agricultural Experiment Station, Lipman said the station had to become more closely connected to the agricultural industry through a statewide extension program—applying scientific research directly to the needs of farmers. According to historian Ingrid Nelson Waller, Lipman's tenure as director of the station was, "in fact, the beginning of a new era in the station's life, marked by an enlarged and balanced program of inspection service, research and extension."[17] On the occasion of the station's fiftieth anniversary in 1930, it was said of Lipman that "his vision of what things should be was, fortunately, augmented by his willingness to do yeoman service to bring those things to pass. But what more could such a man wish to have said of him than that he devoted his whole life to making his state a better place to live in—better for the farmer, for the business and professional [person,] for the laborer—for all the people."[18]

Seventy-five years later, farmland is being preserved, farmers still go into their fields from sunup to sundown, and the labels Jersey Fresh, Jersey Grown, and Jersey Organic stand for high-quality agricultural products. Despite many and often severe pressures, and with the considerable assistance of the Agricultural Experiment Station that Lipman championed, the state of the gardens of the Garden State in this first decade of the twenty-first century is good.

"Either Change ❧ CHAPTER 7
and Keep Up
or Get Out
of the Way"

The New Jersey Farm Bureau, which celebrates eighty-seven years in 2006 and occupies a nineteenth-century building across the street from the State House in Trenton, is very much twenty-first century. Peter Furey, the executive director, sat at the long table in the Bureau's boardroom one morning and predicted that the gardens of the Garden State will survive and prosper if New Jersey farmers can make the transition from a past where they simply raised a crop and "expected someone to come along and buy it" to a future where they will "assess the marketplace, find a niche they can fill, and then go after that niche."

What Furey and others, including Agriculture Secretary Charles Kuperus, are recommending is nothing less than a radical departure from business as usual, the usual in this case being what New Jersey farmers have practiced pretty much since they took over the land from the Leni-Lenape women four hundred years ago. For most of those centuries, Garden State farms, bountiful as they were, raised their crops primarily for purchase in bulk by the great markets of New York and Philadelphia, and, to a lesser extent,

Boston and some overseas. Particularly in the middle years of the twentieth century, much of the annual harvest was also under contract to the giant processing plants that dotted the southern counties. Garden State farmers now have to find new ways to sell themselves and their products. "We have to learn how to deal directly with consumers," said Shirley Kline of Stow Creek Township, Cumberland County. "We have to merchandise." She and her husband, Wesley, Cumberland County agriculture agent, own Happy Valley Berry Farm and sell nearly all their berries directly to farm markets.

🌸 *Farmers Find Their Niche*

The evidence strongly suggests that an increasing number of farmers are following Furey's, Kuperus's and Kline's advice. As usual, their efforts are encouraged and aided by the federal and state Departments of Agriculture, the Farm Bureau, and the Rutgers Agricultural Experiment Stations. Especially helpful when it comes to helping farmers also to become entrepreneurs is the Food Innovation Center in Bridgeton, Cumberland County, one of the Agricultural Experiment Stations. The Food Innovation Center is, in part, a response to research conducted in 1997 by Adesoji Adelaja, then executive dean of Cook College. He concluded that New Jersey farmers, whose farms are smaller than most of those in the rest of the country (an average 83 acres compared to 441 acres) and who pay among the highest prices for land and labor, will remain competitive only if they can find new, innovative ways to market their products. According to Diane D. Holtaway, the center's associate director for business development, those innovative ways include whatever it takes to add value to an agricultural product. "By adding value, I mean taking that step or those steps that will make an agricultural product more appealing to the consumer or buyer. It might mean, for example, picking apples off the tree and making apple pies or slicing the apples for dipping."

Or making peach cider. One of the Food Innovation Center's successful clients to date is Santo John Maccherone, the third generation owner of Circle M Farms located in Harrison Township, Gloucester County. Every summer from 1942 to 2002, Circle M

Farms threw away as much as 10 percent of its peach crop because there was no market for too-ripe fruit. Then Maccherone got an idea that began with two questions: Could the sweet juice of over-ripe peaches be turned into a beverage, and would anybody want to drink it? He took his idea/questions to the Food Innovation Center, where the staff helped supply answers: Yes, peach juice could become peach cider, and it could be bottled by a processor down south that the staff was aware of; yes, it could be initially marketed to consumers through farmers' markets and roadside stands, and it might be smart to offer free samples to people who couldn't imagine cider being made from anything other than apples. "Without the center's help, I wouldn't have been able to follow up on my idea," said Maccherone. "Now, I don't throw away any peaches." In the first year of production, Maccherone sold seven thousand gallons of his Circle M Peach Cider Beverage in sixteen-ounce and half-gallon bottles. In 2006, Maccherone expects to double production, and he is already thinking about bottling the peach cider beverage himself in a couple of years. "I might even add nectarine cider."

Maccherone may indeed build his own bottling facility someday, but he may first take advantage of equipment that the Food Innovation Center hopes to include in its planned 23,000-square-foot business incubator in Bridgeton. According to the Summer 2005 issue of *The Innovator*, a center publication, "a broad range of companies will benefit from this new facility, from fledgling startups in need of basic small scale processing capacity to sophisticated businesses in need of pilot or test market processing for new product development. The small operator will gain access to otherwise unaffordable equipment and services. Larger processors will minimize the capital risks associated with new products and processes in test market, scale up or commercialization phases."

The incubator will feature space for cold assembly and processing where, for example, farmers might employ workers to clean, cut, and bag assorted fresh vegetables for direct sale to consumers. People may now go into any number of fast-food establishments, such as Wawa stores, and purchase fresh fruit in small plastic containers. There is no reason why New Jersey fruit farmers couldn't put together those kinds of containers in the incubator, said Holtaway. Such containers would be value-added products. Next to the cold assembly and processing facilities will be areas for hot assembly and processing where, for example, farmers might turn some of their products into soups or stews. According to *The Innovator*, a client services area "will include a product development research kitchen, microbiology and analytical laboratories, a consumer research/focus group center, conference and education facilities, and office/administrative support." The center needs nearly $9 million to build the incubator, said Holtaway. In the fall of 2005, the center had raised slightly less than $6 million. Funding has come from a number of federal, state, and local sources, including the New Jersey Casino Reinvestment Development Authority.

Of course, as Santo Maccherone and more than two hundred other center clients from all twenty-one counties can attest, the center is not biding its time waiting for the incubator to be built. Andrew Law, New Jersey director for the U.S. Department of Agriculture (USDA) Rural Development program, which actively encourages value-added projects, believes the center may be one of a kind in the nation. "It shows how farming in urban states can succeed if the necessary changes are made," he has stated. "The New Jersey model can work for other states where farmers are experiencing similar cultural and economic pressures."[1] Law also has been quoted by the Associated Press as stating that the value-added concept and niche marketing "might be the last chance for the survival of agriculture in the state."

Penni Heritage of Heritage Station Vineyards & Winery in Richwood, Gloucester County, would agree. "We felt we had a very good idea to convert some of our orchards into vineyards," said Heritage. "We learned how to make wine [with the help of the center], produced our first bottles in 2000, and won awards from the beginning. [Then], we needed to hire a winemaker, expand facilities, and boost our marketing to ensure our growth. The Food Innovation Center coached us every step of the way through a very complex application for a USDA value-added grant. As a result, we received a $50,000 grant. Without [the center's] help, I know we wouldn't have succeeded, and without our value-added products we would not be surviving in farming today."

Another satisfied client of the Food Innovation Center is the Sussex County Cooperative Milk Producers Association. Over the last six years or so, the dairy industry in New Jersey has significantly declined. The number of milk cows, for example, decreased from nineteen thousand in 1998 to thirteen thousand in 2003, and gross income dropped precipitously during the same period from $45 million to a little over $27 million. To the rescue came the Food Innovation Center, which, according to Peter Southway of the Sussex County Cooperative Milk Producers Association, "helped us look at the huge dairy industry, analyze it step by step, and apply the principles of a large, complex marketplace to our small niche." The association's niche is actually not so small. It involves eighteen dairy farmers in Sussex County and northern Warren County whose ambition it is to begin bottling in 2006 high-quality, Jersey Fresh milk. When the association talks quality, Southway said, that means that its milk will have no more than 300,000 parts bacteria in a million pounds of milk as compared to the national average of 500,000 and the 750,000 parts allowed by federal law. Initially, the milk will be bottled by a company in Newark according to very strict standards set by the cooperative, said Southway, but the dairy farmers may eventually buy or build their own plant closer to their farms. "Oh, we're also going to make cheeses," said Southway. "That's more value added."

Cedar Run Farms in Pittsgrove, Salem County, the same Walker family business that sells quality asparagus seed developed by the Rutgers Agricultural Experiment Station in Bridgeton (see Chapter Six), turned to the Food Innovation Center for help in marketing its new Espárrago brand of asparagus guacamole and asparagus salsa. Cedar Run Farms' niche enables it to profit from products that have added value above and beyond the value of the fresh asparagus spears it normally sells at its roadside market. The company Web site's smart promotion for the guacamole and salsa is obviously pitched to today's weight and health conscious Americans: "fat free, low sodium and carbs." Scott Walker's message to other New Jersey farmers who may be content with very old ways in very new and challenging times: "Either change and keep up or get out of the way."

Another example of the kind of niche marketing and value-added innovations that are defining the future for New Jersey's agriculture industry is Dalponte Farms in Richland, Atlantic County. Up until a few years ago, Dennis Dalponte senior grew exactly what his grandfather—and most farmers in the area—had always grown: tomatoes, peppers, and asparagus. Then, one evening he happened to tune in the food channel on television and learned that the best chefs use lots of herbs in cooking and garnish their fancy entrees, salads, and desserts with mint. Not long after, he and sons Dennis junior and Doug replanted one hundred acres in herbs, leeks, and collards and thirty acres of mint. The Dalponte mint is sold under the trade name Mr. Mint to markets along the East Coast and as far west as Chicago. Dennis junior admits that thirty acres of mint don't come close to matching the much larger spreads in some western states, "but I think most of those big outfits sell their mint for oil to be used in jelly and chewing gum." According to Dennis junior, most of Mr. Mint winds up as garnish in mojitos, a popular drink featured by Bacardi's rum and served in posh bars from Miami Beach to New York City. As a promotional stunt in the summer of 2005, Bacardi had its flying bat logo cut into the Delponte mint field like a maze. "We had helicopters flying over us taking pictures," said Dennis junior. An earlier Bacardi promotion for mojitos and Mr. Mint, arranged by a New York public relations firm, included signs along Route 40 that welcomed drivers to fictional Mojito rather than to the real Buena Vista Township (which includes Richland). The Township Committee allowed the two-week promotion because, according to Mayor Chuck Chiarello's public statement at the time, "we have a very large farming community here, and we thought this [promotion] would support it."

In the spring of 2004, Jack Rabin, associate director for farm services at Rutgers Cooperative Extension Service, arranged with Riviera Produce in Englewood, Bergen County (where Dutch farmers tilled the soil in the 1600s), to establish a connection between New Jersey farmers and restaurants, private clubs and corporate dining rooms in New Jersey, lower New York State, and southern Connecticut. A few farmers who sell to Riviera Produce are in Bergen and adjacent counties, said Ben Friedman, owner of Riviera

Produce, but he buys primarily from farming cooperatives in south Jersey. "There just aren't enough farms left up here," he said. "You need a lot of land, and most of the land is down south." By the end of the 2005 harvest, Riviera Produce was purchasing three thousand to four thousand cases of produce a week. Most of the vegetables and fruits come from the Landisville Produce Coop in Atlantic County, which represents 150 farmers. Writing about the program, Linda A. Johnson, business writer for the Associated Press, said the program begun by Rabin is still another way "to help the state's farmers stay in business despite high operating costs, encroaching development, and big distributors [who often give] preference to cheaper produce from [other states and countries]."[2]

Five South Jersey farmers have joined together to market their crops directly to supermarkets, restaurants, food processors like Ready Pac, and even to local fast food chains such as Papa John's Pizza. Eastern Fresh Growers, located in Cedarville, Cumberland County, is under the direction of Tom Sheppard of Sheppard Farms, one of the growers that founded the company. The farmers represented need not wait around for someone to come along and offer a price for their produce, which may be far lower than what they wanted or needed, said Sheppard. "That's like going to Atlantic City and hoping you're going to hit big. Ours is a sure hit." Typically, he said, Eastern Fresh Growers arranges for sales of produce even before the crops have been harvested. "We tell buyers what we're going to have and when and what price we want for the stuff. We have more clout that way." Sheppard is a college graduate whose major was business management and marketing. "Farmers today have to be businessmen."

One of the farmers that sells produce through Eastern Fresh Growers is Tommy Sorbello of Woolwich Township, Gloucester County. His seven hundred acres of tomatoes, peppers, asparagus, cucumbers, and cantaloupes make his farm one of the largest in the state, where the average size is less than one hundred acres. Sorbello's operation also is ideal for Eastern Fresh Growers because he is one of a few farmers who precool their vegetables before they go to market. "This keeps them fresher," he said. Echoing Peter Furey's statement about the way farmers approached the marketplace in decades gone by, Sorbello said, "Eastern Fresh

Growers is a way for farmers to stabilize the market a little bit instead of us having to take our produce somewhere and hope somebody will buy it." When Sorbello's father started farming with 150 acres in 1936, he shared the marketplace mostly with other farmers in the Garden State and those in a fairly narrow ring around Philadelphia and New York. "Today, we're competing with farmers from all over the world." Businesses like Eastern Fresh Growers help local farmers survive and even win in the competition.

At the same time dozens of small farmers from Sussex to Cape May and from Bergen to Salem are experimenting with and embracing niche farming and direct merchandising to consumers, several major segments of the agriculture industry are engaged in expansion and innovation. They are biotechnology, aquaculture, and winemaking. Just as important, perhaps, is a still small but growing trend toward tunnel farming, a European import that could extend the growing season for many Garden State farmers by three to five months.

✻ *Your Car May Run on Jersey Corn and Soybeans*

One spring day in 2005, David Specca, director of the Rutgers Eco-Complex, in Bordentown, Burlington County, handed me tomatoes ripened in a greenhouse powered year-round by gases from the nearby Burlington County landfill while he talked about reducing gasoline consumption by making ethanol from Jersey corn. At the same time, some downstate farmers were driving tractors powered by biodiesel fuel made primarily from soybeans. That's biotechnology, or, as some refer to the science, environmental technology.

According to a report by the Woodrow Wilson Foundation's Biology Institute, "Biotechnology at the beginning of the Twentieth Century began to bring industry and agriculture together. During World War I, fermentation processes were developed that produced acetone from starch and paint solvents for the rapidly growing automobile industry. Work in the 1930s was geared toward using surplus agricultural products to supply industry instead of imports or petrochemicals. Biotechnology is currently being used in many areas, including agriculture . . . food processing, and energy production."[3]

Ethanol, an example of biotechnology's impact on energy production, is already added to gasoline in nineteen states, according to the Renewable Fuels Association, and the New Jersey Farm Bureau and state Department of Agriculture are actively promoting the establishment of an ethanol plant in this state. At the end of 2005, it seemed certain the plant would be built the next year in Deptford Township, Gloucester County, by Garden State Ethanol. It is a little known fact, Specca said, that Henry Ford originally designed his Model T Ford to run on ethanol. "Ethanol actually has a higher octane than gasoline. Ethanol by itself is one hundred sixteen octane, so when you combine it with gasoline, it improves the spark—the octane rating." The technology over the last thirty years has made it possible to produce ethanol more cheaply and also more environmentally friendly, said Specca. "Today it is cost competitive and also energy positive. At one point it took more energy to make it than you got out of it, but that's not the case anymore. Corn yields have improved and the efficiency of ethanol plants has improved. Now, for every one hundred BTUs of energy put in, you get one hundred and sixty-seven out." Also, ethanol production reduces greenhouse gases, because ethanol production recycles carbon dioxide. "The corn, when it's growing, takes carbon dioxide out of the air to make the corn kernel, and when the corn is turned into ethanol, the ethanol produces carbon dioxide that then goes back into the corn."

"Fuel from renewable sources is finally taking off in the United States, and New Jersey should be no exception," stated Richard Nieuwenhuis, president of the New Jersey Farm Bureau, which supports Garden State Ethanol. "Wouldn't it be a good thing to not only reduce our dependence on foreign oil . . . but also be able to produce energy that is renewable within our own state, while benefiting our farmers and the public at large in the process? Research presented by the New Jersey Department of Agriculture shows that the proposed ethanol plant is projected to use 14.5 million bushels of corn per year to generate forty million gallons of ethanol, and the distilling process would also produce 121,000 tons of distilled grains for use as livestock feed."[4] Not at all incidentally, the use of ethanol as an additive to gasoline could, based on other states' experience, save New Jersey drivers twenty to thirty cents a gallon.

Specca, who grew up on his family's vegetable farm in Burlington County, believes that converting corn into ethanol is a promising way to help Garden State farmers, especially now that the state, counties, and municipalities are investing millions of dollars into farm preservation. "We have to come up with businesses that will keep those [preserved] farms operating profitably."

Another such profitable business may be the production of biodiesel fuel from soybeans. In 2005, nearly 100,000 New Jersey acres were planted in soybeans, and more than thirty farmers and assorted companies and organizations in the state, including the Medford School District, were using some blend of processed soybean oil and diesel fuel in their equipment. Also in that year, Woodruff Energy in Cumberland County was the major distributor of biodiesel fuel, which was produced by a Massachusetts company.

According to the Maryland Soybean Board, which actively promotes the use of biodiesel fuel in the mid-Atlantic states, biodiesel is "a clean-burning alternative fuel for diesel engines . . . that is simple to use, biodegradable, nontoxic and essentially free of sulfur and aromatics. Biodiesel is not raw vegetable oil. It is produced by a chemical process that removes glycerin from the oil."[5] In the summer of 2005, BJ Farms in Cumberland County, which grows soybeans, was using a 5 percent blend of biodiesel fuel supplied by Woodruff Energy in all of its off-road farm equipment. Speaking for BJ Farms, Frank Baitinger was quoted as saying that biodiesel fuel "burns cleaner, and it is much more environmentally friendly. We also think our equipment produces less noise when we start it up." The only drawback, Baitinger stated, is the higher cost of biodiesel fuel. It was costing BJ Farms about four cents a gallon more than regular diesel fuel. However, he added that, "while we have not proven any cost savings yet, we feel this product is more about supporting our own industry and the equipment being more efficient."[6]

The Maryland Soybean Board quoted Joe Bilock, Jr., as saying that the Medford School District in Burlington County has been using a mix of 20 percent biodiesel fuel and 80 percent petroleum in twenty of its school buses since 1997. "It's been absolutely fantastic," stated Biluck, who is the district's director of operations.

"We've had no down time as a result of this fuel. We've seen no drop in miles per gallon, which means the engines aren't working any harder. We've run down to temperatures of eleven degrees below zero and haven't experienced any problems." Just as importantly, stated Biluck, students riding the buses, including disabled children, experience less irritation from fumes.[7]

In June 2006, federal regulations that significantly reduce the amount of sulfur in diesel fuel became effective, said Furey. That action, coupled with ever higher costs for petroleum, will increase the demand for biodiesel fuel made from soybeans. He envisions a day, and not very far off, when New Jersey companies will be producing biodiesel fuel from soybeans grown by New Jersey farmers.

⚵ And Now There Is Jersey Seafood

More than twenty years ago, the Garden State decided to call attention to the quality fruits and vegetables grown by its farmers and invented the slogan Jersey Fresh. More recently, the expanding horticulture industry coined the term Jersey Grown. Now, the state Department of Agriculture has added to that lexicon the label Jersey Seafood. However, it shouldn't come as a surprise to the department if many people are just a tad skeptical of the designation. At various times in its history, New Jersey has been known at home and abroad for its tomatoes, asparagus, and blueberries, even turf grass—but surf clams, scallops, and talapia?

Agriculture Secretary Charles M. Kuperus is not surprised. "When people think of New Jersey agriculture, they tend to envision the fertile valleys of the state's northwestern region or the vast acreage of fruits and vegetables spread throughout South Jersey. Perhaps they think of peach orchards in Gloucester County or herds of dairy cows and horse farms. The state's coastal towns don't immediately spring to mind when discussing the overall food and agriculture pictures. But they should." Kuperus points to recent research that indicates "the harvesting of fish and shellfish from open waters and the farming of seafood through aquaculture account for approximately $200 million [paid annually] to the fishermen, and a total contribution to the economy of $600 million."[8] The latest data show that New Jersey is first in the world in the harvesting of surf clams; from 1998 to 2003, the number of pounds of surf clams harvested increased from 44.7 million to 51.3 million pounds. The state also is among the top harvesters of sea scallops, the pounds harvested having increased from 1.6 million in 1998 to 10.6 million in 2003. The value of the scallops harvest was $9.8 million in 1998 and $43.5 million five years later.

New Jersey is, after all, a maritime state and virtually surrounded by water, most of it saline, and the state is dotted with freshwater lakes and streams. Kuperus cites still other data to confirm that the gardens of the Garden State do indeed extend into its bays, rivers, and the Atlantic Ocean. "New Jersey is home to six major ports: Atlantic City, Barnegat Light, Belford, Cape May, Point Pleasant and Port Norris. It might surprise New Jerseyans to learn that Cape May is the sixth largest fishing port in the nation in terms of the value of the catch brought into that port. Last year [2004], over one hundred species of finfish and shellfish were harvested from the waters of the Garden State. More than 1,500 vessels employing nearly 3,000 fishermen call New Jersey home. New Jersey also boasts fifteen seafood processing plants and eighty-one seafood wholesalers, together employing more than 2,300 workers."[9] The state's Aquaculture Development Plan, adopted in 1995, predicts that aquaculture in New Jersey will ultimately create 7,500 jobs and generate $750 million in annual revenue. The plan did not define "ultimately."

In October 2004, the state Department of Agriculture issued its first aquatic farmer license; one year later, the number of licenses had increased to nearly 160. Joseph J. Myers, aquaculture development specialist for the state Department of Agriculture, defines a licensed aquatic farmer as someone who takes some extraordinary steps to enhance the harvest. Such steps might include installing some kind of screen that protects a fishing ground from predators and devising some special means for raising, feeding, or stimulating the growth of finfish or shellfish.

One new licensee is Quality Koi Company in Carneys Point, Salem County. The year 2005 was its first year of full operation. Koi is a Japanese word for carp, an edible freshwater fish by definition, which, in recent years, has come to describe a multicolored ornamental fish sought after by some discerning hobbyists and favored by an increasing number of homeowners who have installed backyard ponds. Quality Koi Company consists of thirty-five outdoor breeding ponds and five greenhouses where upwards of thirty thousand fish may spend the winter before being sold in the early spring, all situated on what was once a forty-two acre asparagus farm now bracketed by U.S. Route 40 and the New Jersey Turnpike. According to Jennifer McCann, office manager, Quality Koi Company is one of only a half dozen such enterprises in the United States, and its customers, many of whom are shops specializing in water gardens, are located in all corners of the country.

The majority of koi raised and sold by the company are less than ten inches long and come in a variety of colors. They ordinarily sell for less than $100 apiece. However, the primary goal for Mathew McCann, company operator, is to raise large red, white, and black carp, each of which may bring thousands of dollars. An exceptionally beautiful twenty-eight-inch specimen bred in 2005 was priced at $50,000, said Jennifer McCann. She compared the fish to a diamond where color and shape are perfect. In the case of the highly prized and highly priced koi, the skin texture was superior and the arrangement of the three primary colors and the colors themselves achieved the status of "living art."

Mathew McCann has been raising koi since he was a seven-year-old boy working for his father in Manchester, England. He came to this country because England has become "saturated" with koi businesses. Nearly every year, he goes to Japan, sometimes accompanied by very valued customers, to learn about new breeding techniques and to select exceptional breeder fish. Some hobbyists, who often belong to koi clubs and attend koi auctions, once had their fish sent from Japan, but shipment costs have increased to the point where that has become impractical. According to Jennifer McCann, fish sold to garden shops and individual customers are first packaged in plastic bags containing just enough water to cover the fishes' gills and enough air to supply oxygen to the water. The sealed bags are then placed in cartons for shipment.

A candidate for licensing as 2005 slipped into 2006 was an as-yet undisclosed organization with international connections (but known to appropriate state officials) that had purchased fifty acres of Cumberland County farmland upon which it plans to construct a modern indoor shrimp farm capable of initially producing annually one million pounds of fresh shrimp. The emphasis is on the word "fresh." According to the organization's general manager, who asked that his name not be revealed when interviewed in early November 2005 because of fierce international competition, the farm will be able to deliver by truck fresh—not frozen—shrimp to any market between Boston and Atlanta within thirty-six hours. It will be the only farm of its kind east of Michigan, said the general manager.

In the spring of 2001, I was in Bivalve, Cumberland County, researching a magazine article about the shipbuilding industry that once bustled along the Delaware Bay and its tributaries. One of my sources was Jack King, who was then seventy-three years old and operating four engine-powered oyster boats. As I was about to leave, King took me up wooden stairs on the side of his shucking shed to look out over the mouth of the Maurice River and the bay beyond, where, in decades past, the tall masts of oyster schooners under sail filled the horizon like a sea of telephone poles. King waved his arm over the near-empty waters and sighed, "It's over, and it won't ever come back." Fortunately, King was wrong.

New Jersey's oyster harvest probably never again will approach what it was in the late nineteenth and early twentieth centuries, but it is far from being over. One who knows is Walter J. Canzonier, president of the New Jersey Aquaculture Association and a longtime fixture at the Haskin Shellfish Research Laboratory, one of the Rutgers Agricultural Experiment Stations, located in Bivalve. In a speech before the Interstate Seafood Seminar in 1992 and in conversation in the summer of 2005, Canzonier acknowledged that the Garden State's oyster industry has been hurt by diseases such as MSX and Dermo and even by some oystermen who unwisely depleted the oyster seed bed in the bay. He also pointed out that the demand for oysters is significantly down from what it was decades ago.

"All of these negative aspects of oyster production would lead the prudent observer to question the viability of the industry in

New Jersey and Delaware Bay in particular. That same prudent observer must, however, recognize a wealth of rather positive evidence that signals the potential for and benefits of producing oysters and other bivalves in New Jersey's estuaries." For one thing, one only needs to walk the corridors of the Haskin Shellfish Research Laboratory with Canzonier and stand behind men and women bent over microscopes to realize that the industry is making headway in its constant battle against diseases that infect oysters. Canzonier was pleased to report in 1992 that the "natural seed beds in the Delaware Bay, the source of small oysters for replanting on the leased grounds in the saltier portions of the estuary . . . have yielded respectable volumes." Furthermore, oysters have reappeared in the Raritan estuary, from which they had "virtually disappeared over fifty years ago."

Canzonier, who has been at work in some capacity at the Haskin Laboratory almost since its beginning in the 1950s (he is now referred to as a visiting scientist), predicts even better days ahead for the oyster industry. "The potential for production is still as great as ever, adverse conditions notwithstanding. Modernization of oyster culture, both in New Jersey and in other East Coast estuaries, will depend in part on the introduction of new technology." One such development, now underway at the Haskin Laboratory, is the discovery and introduction of "parasite tolerant strains of oysters." After showing me around the Haskin Laboratory, Canzonier's parting words were certainly more encouraging than Jack King's four years earlier: "There's still a market for oysters."

✱ The Grapes of Wealth

Diners who desire a glass of fine wine to go with a plateful of Delaware Bay oysters would do well to unplug a bottle of Chardonnay or Riesling produced from grapes grown by any one of New Jersey's twenty-seven licensed wineries. That is more than double the number of wineries just five years ago. For those who were surprised to learn that the Garden State is among the top producers of sea scallops, here is another surprise: New Jersey is fifth among the states in wine production (in order: California, New York,

Washington, Oregon, New Jersey). Before Prohibition temporarily dried out the nation in the 1930s, New Jersey was the number one producer of table wine. Why have so many Garden State farmers converted more than twelve hundred acres of vegetables, orchards and dairies into grape arbors? Tom Sharko, president of the Garden State Wine Growers Association and owner of Alba Vineyard in Finesville, Warren County, has the answer: "Grapes are a high profit crop. One acre of grapes can gross $50,000 to $75,000." Sharko said he receives one or two calls a week from farmers interested in growing grapes for wine. "It's the only economic solution to farmland preservation and preserving open space for farming. There's no other legal crop in the world that can compete."

Writing in *The New Jersey Farmer*, Pegi Ballister-Howells agreed with Sharko. "The cultivation of grapes is not new to the Garden State (the Welch's company, famous for grape juice and jelly, started in the town of Landisville), but the new wine industry may be a key factor in preserving agriculture for the future. There are many reasons for this. Clearly, profitability is most important. If farmers are economically successful, they will not sell their land." She quoted Gary Pavlis, Atlantic County agricultural agent, who pointed out that apple and peach growers, some of whom have been losing money in a depressed market, might do well to consider growing grapes. Apple and peach ground is very suitable for growing grapes, he suggested. Bill and Penny Heritage of Heritage Tree Fruit in Richwood, Gloucester County, were just such peach growers when they decided to try growing grapes. Barrister-Howells described what happened: "[The Heritages] were financially strapped in 2000 when they began converting peach trees to grapes. After only five years, Bill is now farming full time, leaving an off-the-farm job of twenty years. Their nineteen-year-old son, Richard, a student at Cook College, is totally involved in the business and is planning a career as part of Heritage Vineyard. This was all in the nick of time, saving the family farm, which had been producing peaches since 1851."[10]

Jim Quarella, of Bellview Farms in Buena, Atlantic County, was the third generation of his family to grow vegetables, but, he told a newspaper reporter in the summer of 2004, "The prices we were getting for our vegetables and the rising costs of production left no room for profit." Before switching to grapes, Quarella was getting eight dollars for a thirty-pound box of cabbage. In 2004, he was selling a bottle of cabernet sauvignon for fifteen dollars.[11]

New Jersey's climate is conducive to wine growing, according to Sharko, and vineyards are located in all regions of the state, from Westfall Winery in Montague, Sussex County, to Four JG's in Colts Neck, Monmouth County, to Turdo Vineyards in Cape May. Also, growing grapes is not as labor intensive nor as labor expensive as growing some other produce. Jack Tomasello is chairman of the New Jersey Wine Advisory Board and owner of the largest winery in the state at Hammonton, Burlington County. He points out "the need for labor is primarily for the trimming and tying of the vines during the dormant season, when agricultural labor demands are low." Also, harvesting grapes used for wine is done by machine.[12]

Most of the New Jersey wineries sell their product on premises; some of them cater wedding receptions, other parties, and wine-tasting events. The wineries also export their products to other states and even to other countries. Sharko's Alba Vineyard sells wine in eighteen states. The Tomasello Winery in Hammonton is, of course, located in the heart of cranberry and blueberry country, and so his winery produces not only wine made from grapes but also wines made from those other two fruits. According to *The New Jersey Farmer* article, the Tomasello Winery "ships five different fruit wines to nineteen states as well as Japan, Taiwan, South Korea, China, Singapore and, in the near future, Hong Kong."[13]

❊ The Lowdown on High Tunnels

The growing season for Wes and Shirley Kline's raspberries has been extended by nearly four months, and Frank Piazza now starts harvesting tomatoes one or two months before most other farmers in western New Jersey. The reason for the prolonged growing season and for the early harvest is the same: high tunnels. High-tunnel farming is a recent import from Europe, where the technology has benefited farmers in cooler climes. Among those institutions experimenting with and/or promoting high-tunnel farming are Rutgers University, at both Cook College and at its Research and Extension Center in Cumberland County; Penn State University;

and the Virginia Cooperative Extension at Virginia Polytechnic Institute and State University (Virginia Tech).

The high tunnel resembles a greenhouse but is much less costly to build and to operate. The typical tunnel measures seventeen to twenty-one feet in width and thirty-six to forty-eight feet in length. Unlike most permanent greenhouses, the tunnel has a dirt floor rather then concrete or gravel. This allows the farmer to use a small tractor to prepare the soil for planting. A plastic sheet is spread over metal hoops to cover the tunnel. Unlike the typical greenhouse, the tunnel uses neither large, high-powered fans for ventilation nor expensive heating systems. The sidewalls of the plastic sheet can be rolled up to provide ventilation, and the plastic cover allows for retention of solar heat. The only other temperature control might be a standby heater that could be used in early spring if a hard frost threatens.

The tunnels are designed primarily for use by farmers who grow crops on a relatively few acres and whose harvest is targeted for local farm markets and roadside stands. This is true, for example, with both the Klines and Piazza. The Klines, whose farm is in Stow Creek, Cumberland County (Wes Kline is Cumberland County agricultural agent), sell their raspberries in that manner, and Piazza sells most of his tomatoes at his own farmer's market on Route 57 near Phillipsburg in Warren County.

"Not only do high tunnel structures allow farmers to extend their growing season, but they also provide additional benefits," according to Chris Mullins, research specialist for the Virginia Cooperative Extension. "The structures protect crops from the rain, so fungus and disease become less of an issue. The . . . absence of rain allows plants to be grown closer together. [Crops are irrigated by drip tape using tap water.] The [plastic sidewalls] also lower insect pressure. . . . Because insects are less of a problem, pesticides need not be applied as heavily, and farmers may be able to use a natural, biological spray instead."[14] Shirley Kline reported that she and her husband do not use any fungicides and only rarely do they use a pesticide, and that is of an organic type. Most consumers who have eaten fruits or vegetables grown in high tunnels report they taste better than the same fruits or vegetables grown in fields, stated Mullins. "This may be due to the lowered amount of chemicals used in production."[15]

While the dirt floor of the tunnel is seen as an advantage, particularly at the time of planting, it can be a disadvantage if the ground should become contaminated by disease. "Up here [in the northwestern part of the state] we have bacterial canker real bad," said Piazza. In fact, Rutgers used his farm in 2004 as a research project to study the disease and consider how it might be treated. Because he was fearful that his tomatoes could be harmed if planted in soil where the bacterial canker might be present, Piazza tried something different. "I brought in a whole bunch of bags of growing media [consisting primarily of peat moss, perlite, and vermiculite], and we designed a whole system for growing tomatoes in bags. We dropped the bags on the ground, put two holes eighteen inches apart in each bag, and planted two tomatoes in each bag. We put drip tape through the bags, and that was hooked up to an injection system, which supplied water and all the nutrients. Later, we staked and tied up the plants just like we would do in the field." Not only did Piazza harvest an excellent crop of tomatoes from the bags in 2005, he planned to use the same bags for planting tomatoes in the spring of 2006.

Because of high tunnels, the season is longer, the profits greater, and the mood even brighter at Wes and Shirley Kline's Happy Valley Berry Farm on Buckhorn Road in Stow Creek. Before the tunnels, the raspberry harvest started in late June and ended by Halloween. Today, with two of six acres under plastic, the season for picking berries extends from early April to Thanksgiving. "Because of the tunnels," said Shirley Kline, "we have a better quality berry, which has a longer shelf life and brings a higher price." Also, the tunnels' dirt floors have almost no weeds, and without the Klines having to use chemicals. "They're almost as clean as the floors in my house." The Klines plan on adding another five tunnels in the near future.

While high-tunnel farming is bound to play a significant role in the future of the Garden State, Chris Mullins of the Virginia Cooperative Extension predicts the new technique will not replace traditional farming methods. However, high tunnels eventually will nurture many more crops than tomatoes and raspberries. Already, reported Mullins, these other vegetables and fruits have been grown successfully in high tunnels: broccoli, cauliflower, Brussel sprouts, strawberries, various kinds of greens, herbs, and even cherry trees.

✿ *Charting a New Revolution*

Trees. Imagine trillions of new trees growing in every corner of the world, many of them nut trees, perhaps tens of thousands of them dotting New Jersey like leafy sentries forever on guard to protect the Garden State's open space while providing more nourishment for more people. It is not a futuristic pipe dream; it is the hopeful plan proposed by C. Reed Funk, the same farsighted agricultural pioneer who is credited with founding the huge and very profitable turf-grass industry in the state. Funk and his colleague in the Department of Plant Biology and Pathology at Rutgers University, Thomas Molnar, argue for a "New Green Revolution" in which the "widespread use of tree crops will be a primary component."[16] In New Brunswick and Adelphia, Monmouth County, the "New Green Revolution" is already in place. Under Funk's direction, and with the assistance of Rutgers graduate students, twenty thousand nut trees have been planted and are producing.

In the summer of 2005, I sat with Funk in his car parked next to a row of black walnut trees he had planted in Adelphia. He recalled his long association with trees. As a child growing up in Utah in the 1940s, he often sat on the back steps of the family homestead with a handful of apricot pits, which he cracked open and ate. "They tasted a little like almonds. By the way, sweet, pitted apricots are a main source of food in West China, and did you know that one pound of nuts is equal in nutrients to 7.3 pounds of beef?" In addition to black walnut trees, Funk has planted trees bearing Persian walnuts, several varieties of hazelnuts, heartnuts, and pecans. He expects one day to harvest chestnuts in New Jersey. The American chestnut tree, which once prevailed in great numbers in eastern forests and was a primary source of lumber as well as nuts but succumbed to disease in the 1920s, is making a comeback in the Garden State, according to Funk, at least on the grounds of Cook College in New Brunswick.

In their proposal, Funk and Molnar contend that the worldwide planting of nut trees not only would "help ensure adequate supplies of more nutritious and health-promoting food," but at the same time would harvest excess CO_2 from the atmosphere. Trees adapted to land not suitable for sustainable production of cultivated annual crops will produce added food, timber, fuel, and fiber needed to feed, house, and supply energy to the current world's poor and hungry as well as projected population increases in the future. The greatest current and future opportunities exist in the genetic improvement and culture of hundreds of species of underutilized perennial plants, especially tree crops. At Rutgers, we plan to use breeding to increase the usefulness of nut trees as both agricultural and landscape plants. . . . By combining present and continual research efforts and advances with an effective, focused genetic improvement program, it will be possible to develop productive nut tree culture almost anywhere in the world.[17]

In 1987, while conducting research for another book (*Salem County: A Story of People*), I observed members of the Lower Delaware chapter of the Archeological Society of New Jersey digging on the bank of the nearly dry but once lively Two Penny Run. With a properly subdued whoop and holler, they carefully uncovered a hearth upon which, a thousand or more years before there was a place called New Jersey, Leni-Lenape women boiled nuts in water until they could extract their valuable oil. They were living the old green revolution in what was to become the Garden State.

Epilogue 🌟

When I was writing the book *Salem County: A Story of People*, it occurred to me for the first time, I regret to admit, that when the Quakers and the Dutch handed over to the Leni-Lenape a trifling amount of trinkets, the Native Americans were, of course, grateful and were more than willing to share the land, but they didn't figure out until much later—too late, of course—that the tokens they had accepted from the white men had purchased the land they never owned in the first place. All those thousands of acres now belonged to the newcomers, and the Leni-Lenape could continue to use and enjoy the land only insofar as the white settlers allowed.

Years later, while composing this book, from time to time I reflected on those distant transactions and how the Leni-Lenape must have been dumbfounded and not a little angry to learn that those squiggly lines on paper translated "bought and sold," "paid in full." Also occasionally, I imagined little groups of Leni-Lenape women descended from ancient Asian sojourners scratching in gardens where now families with shallow roots in the Garden State live in mammoth, mortgaged mansions.

Fortunately, I also have envisioned Leni-Lenape ghosts hovering above the land they never owned but only tended and offering their guarded approval of how men and women of many races, nationalities, and cultures are today caring for what remains of their and the Europeans' "pleasant and profitable country." Most certainly the ghosts would recognize and delight in the cranberry bogs and acres of blueberries, and they would appreciate that the ocean and rivers and bays are still giving up their clams and scallops and fish, although brightly colored koi would perhaps perplex them. They naturally would smile upon familiar waves of grain. Above all, I submit that the ghosts of Native Americans past would applaud those in places high and low who have conspired and cooperated to preserve land that forever will bring forth vegetables, fruit, grain, and timber and provide pasture and safe haven for assorted domestic animals.

The Leni-Lenape, of course, had no need for planners and designers with strings of professional initials strung out behind their names, but I am confident that if the ghosts were somehow to be reincarnated in the current year, they would quickly latch on to these men and women who contemplate ways to provide housing while safeguarding farmland. "We had our villages," they would say, "and we set aside places where work was performed and places where our people gathered together for ceremonies and conversation. We just knew instinctively that much of the land—most in our time—had to be left to the animals we hunted and the wild berries we picked."

They would quickly see the wisdom of TDR as a good way of accomplishing what they did without zoning maps and master plans. "Your people, like our people, need somewhere to reside," the ghosts come back to life would say, "but they also need open land and the fruits thereof if they are to live healthy and happy as Kishelemukong intended."

At the state Agricultural Convention in February 2006, the Department of Agriculture announced a new advertising campaign designed to freshen the Jersey Fresh slogan and promote at least twenty different fruits and vegetables in season. So, listen up, fellow New Jerseyans and Americans everywhere: the stand-up comedians and detractors are wrong. The gardens of the Garden State are not only alive and well, but flourishing in ways that none of our ancestors could have imagined.

However, I leave you with a warning. At almost any moment, someone somewhere may purposely or inadvertently endanger the centuries-old farming legacy severely and irreversibly. We can't let it happen. The Leni-Lenape ghosts would haunt us forever.

NOTES ✿

CHAPTER 1 "A Pleasant and Profitable Country"

1. Carl Raymond Woodward, "Colonial Agriculture in New Jersey," in *New Jersey: A History*, vol. 1 (New York: American Historical Society, 1930), 265.
2. Ibid., 264.
3. Benson J. Lossing, *Our Country: A Household History* (New York: Henry J. Johnson, 1879), 266.
4. Woodward, "Colonial Agriculture in New Jersey," 268.
5. Ibid.
6. Hubert G. Schmidt, *Agriculture in New Jersey* (New Brunswick: Rutgers University Press, 1973), 46.
7. Lossing, *Our Country*, 272.
8. John E. Pomfret, *The Province of West Jersey: 1609–1702* (Princeton, NJ: Princeton University Press, 1956), 65–71.
9. Ibid.
10. Charles H. Harrison, *Salem County: A Story of People* (Norfolk, VA: Donning, 1988), 20.
11. Schmidt, *Agriculture in New Jersey*, 51.
12. Woodward, "Colonial Agriculture in New Jersey," 272.
13. William A. Whitehead, *East Jersey under the Proprietary Governments* (Newark: Martin R. Dennis, 1875), 314–316.
14. Woodward, "Colonial Agriculture in New Jersey," 278.
15. Ibid., 295 and 296.
16. Bergen County Bar Association, *Washington and His Army in Bergen County* (Hackensack, NJ: Bergen County Bar Association, 1957), 11.
17. Adrian C. Leiby, *The Revolutionary War in the Hackensack Valley* (New Brunswick: Rutgers University Press, 1962), 42.
18. Frances A. Westervelt, *History of Bergen County, New Jersey* (New York: Lewis Historical Publishing), 108.
19. Leiby, *The Revolutionary War in the Hackensack Valley*, 140–141.
20. Ibid., 253.

21. Ibid., 224.
22. Joseph S. Sickler, *The History of Salem County, New Jersey* (Salem, NJ: Sunbeam Publishing, 1937), 35–37.
23. Frank H. Stewart, *Salem County in the Revolution* (Salem, NJ: Salem County Historical Society, 1967), 42.
24. Harrison, *Salem County*, 36.
25. Leiby, *The Revolutionary War in the Hackensack Valley*, 303–304.
26. I. S. Kull, "Agriculture, 1810–1860," in *New Jersey: A History*, vol. 1 (New York: American Historical Society, 1930), 630–631.
27. Ibid.
28. Schmidt, *Agriculture in New Jersey*, 129.
29. Kull, "Agriculture, 1810–1860," 630–631.
30. Sickler, *The History of Salem County, New Jersey*, 198.
31. Schmidt, *Agriculture in New Jersey*, 266.
32. Ron Chernow, *Alexander Hamilton* (New York: Penguin, 2004), 375.
33. Ibid., 373.
34. Ibid., 387.
35. Schmidt, *Agriculture in New Jersey*, 106.
36. Ibid.
37. William Starr Myers, "Agriculture in the State of New Jersey," in *The Story of New Jersey*, ed. W. H. Allen (New York: Lewis Historical Publishing, 1945), 357 and 359.

CHAPTER 2 *"The Biggest Vegetable Factory on Earth"*

1. John T. Cunningham, *Garden State: The Story of Agriculture in New Jersey* (New Brunswick: Rutgers University Press, 1955), 68 and 69.
2. Mary B. Sim, *Commercial Canning in New Jersey: History and Early Development* (Trenton: New Jersey Agricultural Society, 1951), 31.
3. Ibid., 32.
4. North American Phalanx Collection, 1841–1972; Monmouth County Historical Association Library and Archives, Freehold, New Jersey.
5. Sim, *Commercial Canning in New Jersey*, 49 and 50.
6. F. Alan Palmer, *This Place Called Home* (Upper Deerfield, NJ: Upper Deerfield Township Committee, 1985), 120.
7. Ibid., 121.
8. Ibid., 120.
9. Sim, *Commercial Canning in New Jersey*, 247 and 248.
10. *Alloway Remembers* (Alloway, NJ: Alloway Township Bicentennial of the Constitution Committee, 1988), 105.
11. Ibid.
12. Palmer, *This Place Called Home,* 121.
13. Ibid.
14. Charles H. Harrison, *Salem County: A Story of People* (Norfolk, VA: Donning, 1988), 58.
15. Sim, *Commercial Canning in New Jersey*, 148 and 149.
16. Ibid., 154.

17. E. D. McCafferty, *Henry J. Heinz: A Biography* (New York: Bartlett Orr Press, 1923), 58.
18. http://www.heinz.com/jsp/history.jsp.
19. Ibid.
20. McCafferty, *Henry J. Heinz*, 147 and 148.
21. Sim, *Commercial Canning in New Jersey*, 163.
22. Ibid., 164.
23. Edward C. Hampe and Merle Wittenberg, *The Lifeline of America: Development of the Food Industry* (New York: McGraw-Hill, 1964), 120.
24. Ibid.
25. Paul J. Ritter III, "Knights of the Round Tomato: The History of the P. J. Ritter Co., Part 1," *South Jersey Magazine*, Summer 1997, 19.
26. Ibid.
27. Ibid.
28. Paul J. Ritter III, "Knights of the Round Tomato: The History of the P. J. Ritter Co., Part 2," *South Jersey Magazine*, Fall 1997, 15 and 16.
29. Carl Raymond Woodward and Ingrid Nelson Waller, *New Jersey's Agricultural Experiment Station* (New Brunswick: New Jersey Agricultural Experiment Station, 1932), 25, 26, and 34.
30. Cunningham, *Garden State*, 74 and 75.
31. Ingrid Nelson Waller, *Where There Is Vision* (New Brunswick: Rutgers University Press, 1955), 56 and 57.
32. Ibid., 57 and 58.
33. Hubert G. Schmidt, *Agriculture in New Jersey* (New Brunswick: Rutgers University Press, 1973), 266.
34. *The Canning Trade*, September 14, 1970, 19.
35. "Biggest Vegetable Factory on Earth," *Life* magazine, January 3, 1955, 41.
36. Cunningham, *Garden State*, 59.
37. John M. Seabrook, *The Henry Ford of Agriculture* (Upper Deerfield, NJ: Seabrook Educational and Cultural Center, 1995), 25.
38. Charles H. Harrison, *Growing a Global Village: Making History at Seabrook Farms* (New York: Holmes and Meier, 2003), 89.
39. Seabrook, *The Henry Ford of Agriculture*, 46.
40. Ibid., 52.
41. Harrison, *Growing a Global Village*, 129.
42. Frank S. Kelland and Marilyn C. Kelland, *New Jersey: Garden or Suburb?* (Dubuque, IA: Kendall/Hunt Publishing, 1978), 137.
43. Paul J. Ritter III, "Knights of the Round Tomato: The History of the P. J. Ritter Co., Part 5," *South Jersey Magazine*, Summer 1998, 24.
44. Ibid., 25.
45. Ibid.
46. Ibid.
47. Ron LeHew, "Autumn Brings Familiar Aroma to County," *Today's Sunbeam*, October 17, 2004, A3.
48. Harrison, *Growing a Global Village*, 144.

CHAPTER 3 *"A Decent Home for Every American Family"*

1. Barbara M. Kelly, "The Houses of Levittown in the Context of Postwar American Culture," in *Preserving the Recent Past,* ed. Deborah Slaton and Rebecca A. Schiffer (Washington, DC: Historic Preservation Education Foundation, 1995), 4.
2. Ibid., 2.
3. *1940 Yearbook of Agriculture: Farmers in a Changing World* (Washington, DC: U.S. Government Printing Office, 1940), 382.
4. Raymond M. Ralph, *Bergen County, New Jersey: History and Heritage,* vol. 6, *Farmland to Suburbia* (Hackensack, NJ: Bergen County Board of Chosen Freeholders, 1983), 64.
5. Ibid., 65.
6. Thomas J. Hooper, "Paramus: Town with a Future," *Newark Sunday News,* September 28, 1952, 12 and 13.
7. Frederick W. Bogert, *Paramus: A Chronicle of Four Centuries* (Paramus, NJ: Paramus Free Public Library, 1961), 124.
8. Hooper, "Paramus," 12.
9. "Planning Essay," *Growth Management Overview,* vol. I, *Bergen County Cross Acceptance Report to the State Planning Commission* (Hackensack, NJ: Bergen County Department of Planning and Economic Development, 1989), 2–12, 2–13, and 2–15.
10. David Halberstam, *The Fifties* (New York: Villard Books, 1993), 133.
11. Carol J. Cunningham Suplee, *Stories of Willingboro Township, New Jersey* (Willingboro, NJ: Calkins Newspapers, 1991), 74.
12. Herbert L. Gans, *The Levittowners: Ways of Life and Politics in a New Suburban Community* (New York: Pantheon Books, 1967), 5.
13. Hubert G. Schmidt, *Agriculture in New Jersey* (New Brunswick: Rutgers University Press, 1973), 237.
14. Suplee, *Stories of Willingboro Township, New Jersey,* 85.
15. Tyson Freeman, "The 1950s: Post-war America Hitches Up and Heads for the 'Burbs," *National Real Estate Investor,* September 20, 1999, 3.
16. Suplee, *Stories of Willingboro Township, New Jersey,* 104.
17. Tracy Duffield, "The Way We Live in New Jersey," *Farm and Ranch Living,* December/January 2005, 10.
18. "The New Jersey Agricultural Situation," Report of the Blueprint Commission on the Future of New Jersey Agriculture, April 1973, 8.
19. William H. Whyte, *The Last Landscape* (New York: Doubleday, 1968), 23.

CHAPTER 4 *"Keep Farmers Farming"*

1. Frank S. and Marilyn C. Kelland, *New Jersey: Garden or Suburb?* (Dubuque, IA: Kendall/Hunt Publishing, 1978), 134.
2. George W. Luke, *Actively Devoted: The First Decade of the New Jersey Farmland Assessment Act* (Trenton: New Jersey Farmland Evaluation Advisory Committee, 1976), 2–4.
3. Ibid., 5.
4. Kelland, *New Jersey,* 134.

5. *Grassroots: An Agriculture Retention and Development Program for New Jersey* (New Jersey Department of Agriculture, 1980), 8.
6. Ibid., 8 and 9.
7. Walter F. Naedele, "Agricultural Meeting Lures Farmer from Wintry Repose," *Philadelphia Inquirer*, January 27, 1983, B1.
8. Robert E. Coughlin, John C. Keene, J. Dixon Esseks, William Toner, and Lisa Rosenberger, *National Agricultural Lands Study: The Protection of Farmland* (Washington, DC: U.S. Government Printing Office, 1981), 4.
9. Tom Daniels and Deborah Bowers, *Holding Our Ground: Protecting America's Farms and Farmland* (Washington, DC: Island Press, 1997), 176.
10. Ibid., 171 and 172.
11. Michele S. Byers, *TDR—Your Town's New Tool to Fight Sprawl* ("State We're In" column, March 31, 2004), reprinted in *Sierra Activist*, January 7, 2005.

CHAPTER 5 *"We Sure Hope It Works"*

1. Michele S. Byers, "Developers Getting Old McDonald's Tax Breaks," *Sierra Activist*, May 5, 2004.
2. James Howard Kunstler, *Home from Nowhere: Remaking Our Everyday World in the 21st Century* (New York: Simon and Schuster, 1996), 110.
3. William H. Whyte, *The Last Landscape* (New York: Doubleday, 1968), 24.
4. Andres Duany, Elizabeth Plater-Zyberk, and Jeff Speck, *Suburban Sprawl* (New York: North Point Press, 2000), 110.
5. "Salem County's Future," *Today's Sunbeam*, Salem, June 1, 2004, A4.
6. "Preservation: Time Is Running Out," *Today's Sunbeam*, Salem, November 2, 2003, A6.
7. "Another Family Forced to Abandon Farming," *Today's Sunbeam*, Salem, July 17, 2005, A6.

CHAPTER 6 *"Always a Call to the Land"*

1. Frederick V. Coville, "The Wild Blueberry Tamed," *National Geographic*, June 1916, 535.
2. Frederick V. Coville, "Early Experiments with Blueberries," USDA Bulletin No. 974, Washington, DC, October 15, 1921, 1.
3. Coville, "The Wild Blueberry Tamed," 546.
4. Ibid.
5. Ingrid Nelson Waller, *When There Is Vision* (New Brunswick: Rutgers University Press, 1955), 68.
6. Ibid.
7. Paul Eck, *The American Cranberry* (New Brunswick: Rutgers University Press, 1990), 2.
8. Ibid.
9. Ibid., 5.

10. Raymond J. Samulis, "Growing Cranberries in New Jersey," http://www.rcc.rutgers.edu/burlington/cranberr.htm, July 21, 2005, 6.
11. Official Proceedings of the Thirty-second Meeting of the American Cranberry Growers' Association, Bingham Hotel, Philadelphia, January 28, 1902.
12. "NJTA History," http://www.njturfgrass.org.
13. Ibid.
14. "New Jersey Department of Agriculture Kicks Off 'Jersey Grown,'" *New Jersey Farmer*, May 1, 2005, 3.
15. Mike Azzara, "Turkey to Be Thankful For," NOFA-NJ's *Organic News*, vol. 18, no. 4, Fall 2004, 1.
16. Ibid., 6.
17. Waller, *When There Is Vision*, 90.
18. Ibid., 12.

CHAPTER 7 *"Either Change and Keep Up or Get Out of the Way"*

1. Jeanne Ridgway, "Agribusinesses Change Their Ways," Annual Business Review, *Courier-Post*, June 10, 2005.
2. Linda A. Johnson, "Program Helps New Jersey Farmers Thrive," Associated Press News Service, September 14, 2004.
3. Ann Murphy and Judy Perrella, "A Further Look at Biotechnology" (Princeton, NJ: The Woodrow Wilson Foundation Biology Institute, 1993), 1.
4. "NJ Farm Bureau Urges Adoption of Ethanol as Gasoline Additive," *New Jersey Farmer*, March 15, 2005, 1.
5. "What Is Biodiesel Fuel?" *SOY Biodiesel in the News*, Maryland Soybean Board, 2005, 1.
6. Jaime Marine, "Future Fuel Comes to South Jersey," *Today's Sunbeam*, July 28, 2005, 22.
7. "What Is Biodiesel Fuel?" 10.
8. Charles M. Kuperus, "Efforts Abound to Promote New Jersey's Delicious Seafood Products," http://www.jerseyseafood.nj.gov/seafoodopedPR.htm, September 12, 2005.
9. Ibid.
10. Pegi Ballister-Howells, "A Crushing Need for Grapes," *New Jersey Farmer*, April 15, 2005, 1.
11. Suzette Parmley, "The Grapes of Redemption," *Philadelphia Inquirer*, June 6, 2004, B1.
12. Howells, "A Crushing Need for Grapes," 2.
13. Ibid.
14. "High Tunnel Structures Offer a New Tool for Farmers," Virginia Cooperative Extension, March 4, 2004.
15. Ibid.
16. C. Reed Funk and Thomas Molnar, "Genetically Improved Tree Crops: Key to Continuing the Green Revolution," unpublished manuscript, May 2005, 1.
17. Ibid.

INDEX

ABOUT THE AUTHOR

Charles H. Harrison has made his home in New Jersey all his life, first in Bergen County and now in Salem County. He is the author or coauthor of nine nonfiction books. Two are about New Jersey history: *Salem County: A Story of People* (1988) and *Growing a Global Village: Making History at Seabrook Farms* (2003). He also has written a number of articles about New Jersey history and teaches a course in magazine article writing at Rowan University in Glassboro.